W9-BVC-512

Pedagogy of Freedom

Critical Perspectives Series

Series Editor: Donaldo Macedo, University of Massachusetts, Boston
A book series dedicated to Paulo Freire

Critical Education in the New Information Age by Manual Castells, Ramón Flecha, Paulo Freire, Henry A. Giroux, Donaldo Macedo, and Paul Willis

Critical Ethnicity: Countering the Waves of Identity Politics edited by Robert H. Tai and Mary L. Kenyatta

Debatable Diversity: Critical Dialogues on Change in American Universities by Raymond V. Padilla and Miguel Montiel

Imagining Teachers: Rethinking Gender Dynamics in Teacher Education by Gustavo E. Fischman

Immigrant Voices: In Search of Educational Equity edited by Enrique (Henry) T. Trueba and Lilia I. Bartolomé

Latinos Unidos: From Cultural Diversity to the Politics of Solidarity by Enrique (Henry) T. Trueba

Pedagogy of Freedom: Ethics, Democracy, and Civic Courage by Paulo Freire

Pedagogy, Symbolic Control, and Identity, revised edition, by Basil Bernstein

A Sanctuary of Their Own: Intellectual Refugees in the Academy by Raphael Sassower

Sharing Words: Theory and Practice of Dialogic Learning by Ramón Flecha

Forthcoming

Ideology Matters by Paulo Freire and Donaldo Macedo

Paulo Freire and the Social Imagination: From Dreams to Praxis by Maxine Greene

Pedagogy of Freedom

Ethics, Democracy, and Civic Courage

PAULO FREIRE

TRANSLATED BY PATRICK CLARKE
FOREWORD BY DONALDO MACEDO
INTRODUCTION BY STANLEY ARONOWITZ

ROWMAN & LITTLEFIELD PUBLISHERS, INC.
Lanham • Boulder • New York • Oxford

ROWMAN & LITTLEFIELD PUBLISHERS, INC.
Published in the United States of America
by Rowman & Littlefield Publishers, Inc.
4501 Forbes Boulevard, Suite 200
Lanham, Maryland 20706
www.rowmanlittlefield.com

12 Hid's Copse Road, Cumnor Hill, Oxford OX2 9JJ, England

Copyright © 1998 by Ana Maria Araujo Freire
First paperback printing 2001.

All rights reserved. No part of this publication may be reproduced, stored in a retrieval system, or transmitted in any form or by any means, electronic, mechanical, photocopying, recording, or otherwise, without the prior permission of the publisher.

British Library Cataloguing in Publication Information Available

The hardback edition of this book was catalogued by the Library of Congress as follows:

Freire, Paulo, 1921–1997
    [Pedagogia de autonomia. English]
    Pedagogy of freedom : ethics, democracy, and civic courage / Paulo
Freire ; translated by Patrick Clarke ; foreword by Donaldo Macedo ;
introduction by Stanley Aronowitz.
      p. cm.
    Includes bibliographical references (p.) and index.
    1. Popular education. 2. Critical pedagogy. 3. Teaching.
I. Title
LC196.F73713   1998
370.11'5— dc21   98-30184
                                           CIP

ISBN 0-8476-9046-6 (cloth : alk. paper)
ISBN 0-8476-9047-4 (paper : alk. paper)
ISBN: 978-0-8476-9047-3
Printed in the United States of America

∞™ The paper used in this publication meets the minimum requirements of American National Standard for Information Sciences— Permanence of Paper for Printed Library Materials, ANSI/NISO Z39.48-1992.

To my wife, Ana Maria, with joy and love.

To the memory of Admardo Serafim de Oliveira, to whose serious
and dedicated work I owe much.

To the boys and girls and their teachers of the Axé Project in
Salvador, Bahia, in the person of their tireless and inspired
founder, Cesare de La Roca, with my profound admiration.

CONTENTS

—⁓—

TRANSLATOR'S NOTES

After Paulo Freire's funeral mass, on 3 May 1997, a close friend of mine who was engaged in making a film about Paulo's work came up to me and said, "It's up to us now. We must carry the torch that he has handed to us."

Paulo has been and remains a light in the darkness—the darkness of ideological determinism, fatalism, and organized hopelessness. It is a light that neither persecution, exile, nor unjust criticism has been able to extinguish.

The modest contribution that I am able to make toward keeping the flame alive through this translation came to me unexpectedly—a phone call from Paulo in November 1996, asking if I would do the job. I accepted under protest, first, because translation is not really my field and second, because, in my opinion, there were many people around more qualified to do justice to this work than I myself. His insistence prevailed because, as he said, "you know not only my thought but the soul of the language in which I write." A singular compliment that supplied whatever motivation might have been lacking hitherto.

Indeed, I had been a disciple of Paulo's before I met him, or even knew of him, something to do, perhaps, with having come myself from the ranks of an oppressed people. That discipleship took on a more intensely focused perspective after we met in Paris in 1974, while he was still in exile, and later on his return to Brazil in 1980.

By the time Paulo died, the translation had been two-thirds completed. We had looked at the first third together and he was happy with it. And the last time we spoke, on 30 April 1997, we were making plans to look at the remainder. But that was not to be.

Though I have often wished I could ask him questions or consult him about this or that, I have since relied on his own words, spoken when he asked me to accept a task that I did not really want. Since then I have "labored," trying to reproduce his thought with all the poetic force of enthusiasm, wonder, adventure, and indignation that it possesses as best as I could. In this I feel I have been a faithful and grateful disciple.

As regards the translation of the title, I have opted, after much reflection, for "Pedagogy of Freedom," which seems to possess the resonance required by the text itself. In addition, it haply completes the trilogy of pedagogies, beginning with the "Oppressed" and moving through "Hope" to that place that Paulo so struggled for and desired for everyone he met and that he now enjoys to the full: Freedom. This book is a fitting testament to a noble and ennobling adventure.

Paulo is no longer with us in the way he used to be. And it is hard to become accustomed to his absence. But there is a sense in which he has never gone away. I imagine him sitting quietly, nearby, with a twinkle in his eye, now no longer knowing only "a dim reflection in a mirror," and making his own the words of Joseph Campbell, as he urges us to

say yes to life
yea to it all

and to participate with joy, humility, indignation, and gratitude in the adventurous struggle to remake the world each and every day.

Patrick Clarke
October 1997

FOREWORD

Pedagogy of Freedom was written largely for the graduate seminar on
liberation pedagogy that Paulo Freire and I were scheduled to teach
at the Harvard Graduate School of Education (HGSE) during the
fall semester, 1997. As we were preparing the seminar, Paulo was
overtly concerned with the positivistic overemphasis on the so-called
scientific methods of analysis and absolute objectivity that informs
institutions of higher education, such as the Harvard Graduate School
of Education. The attempts of educators to adopt "hard science"
modes of analysis as part of their research in social sciences have
given rise to a form of "scientism" rather than science. By "scientism"
I refer to the mechanization of the intellectual work cultivated by
specialists, which often leads to the fragmentation of knowledge.
Ortega y Gasset accurately understood this tendency: "A fair amount
of things that have to be done in physics or in biology is mechanical
work of the mind which can be done by anyone, or almost anyone
. . . to divide science into small sections, to enclose oneself in one of
these, and leave out all consideration of the rest."[1] Paulo Freire was
very concerned that institutions like the Harvard Graduate School
of Education were preponderantly supportive of specialists of this
sort who hide their ideology behind a facile call for "scientific rigor"
and "absolute objectivity." These "scientific" educators have often
contributed to a further fragmentation of knowledge because of their
reductionist view of the act of knowing. They repeatedly refuse to
admit to themselves and to others that their claim of objectivity is, in

fact, an ideological act. Objectivity always contains within it a dimension of subjectivity; thus it is dialectical.

Although many educators, particularly those who blindly embrace a positivistic mode of inquiry, would outright deny the role of ideology in their work, nonetheless, they ideologically attempt to prevent the development of any counterdiscourse within their institution. As Freire would point out, if these educators were to claim a scientific posture, for instance, "[they] might try to 'hide' in what [they] regard as the neutrality of scientific pursuits, indifferent to how [their] findings are used, even uninterested in considering for whom or for what interests [they] are working."[2] Because most educators do not really conduct research in the "hard sciences," they uncritically attempt to adopt the "neutrality" posture in their work in the social sciences, leaving out the necessary built-in self-criticism, skepticism, and rigor of hard sciences. In fact, science cannot evolve without a healthy dose of self-criticism, skepticism, and contestation. However, for instance, a discourse of critique and contestation is often viewed as contaminating "objectivity" in social sciences and education. As Freire would argue, these educators "might treat [the] society under study as though [they] are not participants in it. In [their] celebrated impartiality, [they] might approach this real world as if [they] were wearing 'gloves and masks' in order not to contaminate or be contaminated by it."[3]

These metaphorical "gloves and masks" represent an ideological fog that enables educators to comfortably fragment bodies of knowledge. By reducing the intellectual task to pure technicism, they can more easily disarticulate a particular form of knowledge from other bodies of knowledge, thus preventing the interrelation of information necessary to gain a more critical reading of the world. This concern over the technicist approach to education via a reductionist specialization motivated Freire to write *Pedagogy of Freedom,* in which he highlights other fundamental knowledges that all teachers should have, or at least be exposed to, but that are seldom taught to them in their preparation as teachers. He contends that "teaching requires a recognition that education is ideological"; "Teaching always involves ethics"; "Teaching requires a capacity to be critical"; "Teaching requires the recognition of our conditioning"; "Teaching requires humility"; and "Teaching requires critical reflection," among others.

In *Pedagogy of Freedom* Freire convincingly demonstrates that these other fundamental knowledges are absolutely necessary for the development of a critical reading of the world, which implies, according to him, "a dynamic comprehension between the least coherent sensibility of the world and a more coherent understanding of the word."[4] This means, for example, that reading specialists in the United States, who have contributed to a technical advancement in the field of reading, should have the ability to understand and appreciate why millions of children who by virtue of their race, ethnicity, gender, and class have not benefited from these technical advancements and remain illiterate or semiliterate.

Such understanding would invariably necessitate that reading specialists make linkages between their self-contained technical reading methods and the social and political realities that generate unacceptably high failure reading rates among certain groups of students. The making of such linkages would necessarily require courses on the nature of ideology, ethics, and education—courses that are, by and large, missing from the curriculum of schools of education. Although prospective teachers are almost always required, particularly in advanced graduate studies, to take multiple courses in statistics and quantitative research methodologies, no such requirements exist, for example, for a course on the nature of ideology. This very selection process that prioritizes certain bodies of knowledge while discouraging or suffocating other discourses is linked to something beyond education: ideology. Thus, the curriculum selection and organization that favor a disarticulated technical training over courses in critical theory, which would enable students to make linkages with other bodies of knowledge so as to gain a more comprehensive understanding of reality, points to the very ideology that attempts to deny its existence through a false claim of neutrality. The insidious nature of ideology is its ability to make itself invisible.

On May 2, 1997, Paulo Freire died of heart failure. His death unveiled the hidden ideology that informs the conservative corporate empirical focus that shapes the Harvard Graduate School of Education, which reasserted itself when the school canceled the seminar on liberation pedagogy. Rather than affirming Freire's ideas and allowing the seminar to continue, Freire's death suggested that the Harvard Graduate School of Education's interest in his ideas and work was purely a matter of public relations. In other words, it is acceptable to embrace Freire as an icon for one semester to legitimize the Harvard Graduate School of Education's claim of openness, diversity, and democracy, but it is not acceptable to allow his ideas to become part of the general course offerings. Even though Freire has been considered the most important educator in the last half of this century,[5] the Harvard Graduate School of Education does not offer a single course designed specifically to study Freire's theories and ideas. In recent years, a couple of junior, untenured professors who are highly influenced by Freire's ideas have included his work as a part of their reading lists for their courses. However, one cannot comfortably study Freire as part of the general course offerings. The irony is that while the Harvard Graduate School of Education is lukewarm toward Freire's theories and ideas, the Harvard Divinity School offers a course entitled "Education and Liberation" where Freire's work is the central focus.

A few days after Freire's death, I received a telephone call from Dean Monell, the dean for Administration and Academic Services, asking me what I wanted to do with the seminar on liberation pedagogy. I told him that the decision lay with the HGSE administration and faculty but that, nevertheless, I had a proposal. I told him that the best way to honor Freire would be to use the money allocated for Freire's visiting professorship to invite major Freirean scholars, such as bell hooks, Henry Giroux, Stanley Aronowitz, and Ramón Flecha, among others, to come to Harvard and teach a one- or two-week miniseminar on Freire. I offered to coordinate the effort as part of the Seminar on Liberation Pedagogy that I was already scheduled to coteach. I told Dean Monell that my proposal would accomplish at least two things: (1) A symposium of these scholars would, in a significant way, recognize and honor the important contribution to the field of education made by Freire worldwide, and (2) the proposed seminar would expose students at the HGSE to a host of major scholars (both national and international) whose work has not only advanced the theoretical discourse on education but has also contributed enormously to the development of pedagogical structures that link education, liberation, and social justice. Dean Monell's only response to me was that he would present my proposal to the senior faculty members.

Though it took the HGSE administration and faculty many months to respond to Freire's initial proposal that I coteach the Seminar on Liberation Pedagogy with him, the response to my proposal for keeping Freire's ideas alive at the HGSE was immediate, decisive, and to the point. A few days after our initial telephone conversation, Dean Monell left the following message on my answering machine: "This is to tell you that the faculty in the Teaching and Learning Department has decided to cancel the seminar that you were going to coteach with Freire. I have not been able to contact anyone from the David Rockefeller Center for Latin American Studies. It appears that they want to invite another Latin American Scholar. Call me if you have any questions regarding this matter."

I was not surprised that the faculty would cancel the seminar, given the aversion in the culture of the HGSE toward critical theory in general and Freire in particular. This is abundantly clear in an HGSE professor's written comments on a Pepi Leistyna research paper:

> The assumption that ideological sophistication is a sign of cultural progress ignores the fact that many people just don't give a damn about this kind of complex verbalization. They may be temperamentally bent toward building, or singing, or hoeing corn. So the problem for me is to prevent the overinterpretative egghead from claiming a special corner on sacred (significant) knowledge—but still get his or her due. It always makes me a little wary about the extent to which the critical theorists (Freire, Giroux, etc.) appreciate the great range of talents of people who are not so much deluded by all this professional garbage complex elaboration of language. So they often cannot protect themselves, either from specialized professors of literacy or specialized professors of critical literacy.[6]

How can one explain a culture that pontificates about intellectual rigor and yet allows a graduate course titled The Literacy Politics and Policy to be taught without any reference to Freire? The syllabus for this course further revealed its hidden politics: The professor even allotted one week to covering the politics of literacy in Latin America without any reference to Freire. The course also devoted one week to critical literacy without any reference to Freire. In the reading assignments for critical literacy, the most well-known critical literacy authors in the United States, such as Henry Giroux, bell hooks, Linda Brodkey, and Peter McLaren, were also missing. Not requiring students to read Freire in a graduate course on the politics of literacy that covers both literacy in Latin America and critical literacy is tantamount to offering an introduction to linguistics course without mentioning Noam Chomsky or an introduction to British literature course without mentioning Shakespeare. Not only is this evidence of the fear that many professors feel toward Freire's critical theories, but it also points to an extreme level of academic dishonesty and the ahistorical nature of the course. One may not agree with Freire's theories, but one cannot arrogantly ignore the best-known literacy educator in the world. Failure to expose students of literacy to Freire is not only a form of extreme anti-intellectualism but also a de facto censorship. Here is where the HGSE faculty mantra of objectivity and scientific rigor is subverted by a more insidious force: ideology. But what can one expect from a culture in which another professor responded to Freire's death in the following manner: "Freire's coming to Harvard would have made twenty students very happy while making the rest of the students extremely unhappy. Now he is dead and we are all unhappy."

This comment regarding Freire's death not only epitomizes the level of dehumanization and insensitivity that exists at the highest level of education, but it also points to the arrogance (which borders on stupidification) of many professors drawn from the sheer power, resources, and authority of such institutions as Harvard. Many of these professors' identities are tied solely to Harvard's prestige, which gives many of them the illusion that they can dismiss any body of knowledge, views, or perspectives that do not conform to their pre-established ways of seeing the world. In fact, if one applies the rigorous standards of the academy, one soon realizes (1) that, with a handful of exceptions, most of the professors at the HGSE are not among the most-cited educators in the United States, much less in the world, (2) that their work has done little to advance the present theoretical debate in the field, and (3) that they have contributed few earth-shaking ideas that might help to raise schools—particularly urban schools, with their outrageously high dropout rate and high numbers of students who graduate as semiliterates—out of their moribund condition. On the contrary, most of these schools are very much

informed by the positivistic and management models that character-
ize the very culture of ideologies and practices to which Freire was in
opposition all his life.

A permanent feature of the HGSE faculty discourse is the call for
objectivity and scientific rigor; this can be seen, for example, in the
comments on Pepi Leistyna's term paper on the political nature of
bilingual education: "These are unsupported politically motivated
claims! [The professor called for] a more linguistic analysis."[7] As
Leistyna recounts, this same professor told him: "I hope you have
been reading some hard science." When I told this story to Linda
Brodkey, an English professor at the University of California in San
Diego, she laughingly asked: "Why doesn't this professor use her
scientific methods to determine what the scientists in the Harvard
yard think about the scientific research conducted at the Harvard
Graduate School of Education?" She later added that "at best she will
be told that they don't know of any and, at worse, she will be an
object of laughter." By and large, the laughter is justified, because to
a large extent academic work in schools of education is often restricted to derivative analysis in which students, and sometimes professors, are reduced to working with secondary and tertiary texts. Take
the doctorate program in Language and Literacy at the HGSE, for
instance. A student can earn a doctorate in language studies without
any exposure to contemporary linguistic theories. In fact, to my
knowledge, there is not a single course in linguistic theory through
which students could, on the one hand, be exposed to contemporary
theories in the field of linguistics and, on the other hand, develop
tools to understand how theory informs the complex universe of
language use, acquisition, and development. When the suggestion
was made that the program should begin to offer at least a module in
linguistics, the idea was dismissed with the claim that students did
not really need linguistics. Instead, the graduate students in the Language and Literacy Program organized workshops for those students

who come into the program without any knowledge of linguistics. This position not only makes a mockery of the complex field of study that informs all language realizations, but it also points to the atheoretical posture of those professors who hide their anti-intellectualism in the false call for scientific rigor.

Given the anti-intellectual posture of many School of Education professors, a posture that is manifested either through censorship of certain bodies of knowledge or through the disarticulation between the theories of the discipline and the empirically driven and self-contained studies, it becomes obvious why these pseudoscientists

> do not challenge the territorialization of university intellectual activity or in any way risk undermining the status and core beliefs of their fields. The difference, [for scientists,] is that this blindness or reluctance often contradicts the intellectual imperatives of the very theories they espouse. Indeed, only a theorized discipline can be an effective site for general social critique—that is, a discipline actively engaged in self-criticism, a discipline that is a locus for struggle, a discipline that renews and revises its awareness of its history, a discipline that inquires into its differential relations with other academic fields, and a discipline that examines its place in the social formation and is willing to adapt its writing practices to suit different social functions.[8]

As these theoretical requirements make abundantly clear, the decision of the Language and Literacy Program faculty not to expose students to the theoretical linguistics that informs their field of study and the arrogant dismissal of Freire's social critical theories of literacy unveil the ideology behind the prescription that Leistyna should have been "reading some hard science." They expose the almost-illusory and schizophrenic educational practice in which "the object of interpretation and the content of the interpretive discourse are considered appropriate subjects for discussion and scrutiny, but the interests of the interpreter and the discipline and society he or she serves are not."[9]

The disarticulation between the interpretive discourse and the interests of the interpreter is often hidden in the false call for an objectivity that denies the dialectical relationship between subjectivity and objectivity. The false call for objectivity is deeply ingrained in a positivistic method of inquiry. In effect, overemphasis on the school of positivism has resulted in an epistemological stance in which scientism and methodological refinement are celebrated while "theory and knowledge are subordinated to the imperatives of efficiency and technical mastery, and history is reduced to a minor footnote in the priorities of 'empirical' scientific inquiry."[10] Perhaps it is this devaluation of history that enabled a professor at HGSE to tell an international student who is a doctoral candidate "not to cite too many historical sources. In the United States any research that is more than five years old is considered dated." The blind celebration of empiricism has created a culture in which pseudoscientists, particularly in schools of education, who engage in a form of "naive empiricism," believe "that facts are not human statements about the world but aspects of the world itself."[11] According to Michael Schudson,

This view was insensitive to the ways in which the "world" is something people construct by the active play of their minds and by their acceptance of conventional—not necessarily "true" ways of seeing and talking. Philosophy, the history of science, psychoanalysis, and the social sciences have taken great pains to demonstrate that human beings are cultural animals who know and see and hear the world through socially constructed filters.[12]

The same celebration of research methodologies over theory and knowledge led some senior professors at the HGSE to worry that the *Harvard Educational Review* is becoming biased toward publishing critical work that was, according to them, filled with "political rhetoric" rather than research-based scientific articles informed by empirical evidence. Two students on the board of the *Harvard Educational Review* told me that they were reprimanded by some senior professors because they were publishing too many works by Freire, Giroux, Macedo, and Aronowitz, among other critical writers. This not only represents a form of censorship through intimidation, but it is also a distortion of reality because the *Harvard Educational Review* historically has not been in the forefront of publishing critical works. What is really happening is that, through peer review, the works of some senior professors are being rejected while articles by Freire and other critical writers are being published. In other words, these professors seemed to feel that the referee process through peer review could only be considered objective if the process reproduced the dominant ideology and maintained the status quo. This is where the call for objectivity and scientific rigor is subverted by the weight of its own ideology.

What these professors do not realize is that there is a large body of critical literature that interrogates the very nature of what they consider research. Such critical writers as Donna Haraway,[13] Linda Brodkey, Roger Fowler, and Greg Myers, among others, have painstakingly demonstrated the erroneous claim of "scientific" objectivity that permeates all forms of empirical work in social sciences. According to Linda Brodkey, "scientific objectivity has too often and for too long been used as an excuse to ignore a social and hence, political practice in which women and people of color, among others, are dismissed as legitimate subjects of research."[14] The blind belief in objectivity not only provides pseudoscientists with a safe haven from which they can attempt to prevent the emergence of counterdiscourses that interrogate "the hegemony of positivism and empiricism," [15] but also generates a form of folk theory concerning objectivity believed only by nonscientists. In other words, as Linda Brodkey so eloquently put it, "any and all knowledge, including that arrived at empirically, is necessarily partial, that is, both an incomplete and an interested account of whatever is envisioned." [16] In fact, what these pseudoscientists consider research, that is, work based on quantitative evaluation results, can never escape the social construction that generated these models of analysis. The theoretical concepts are always shaped by the pragmatics of the society that devised these evaluation models in the first place. [17] That is, if the results are presented as facts that were originally determined by a particular ideology, these facts cannot in themselves illuminate issues that lie outside of the ideological construction of these facts to begin with. [18] I would warn educators that these evaluation models can provide answers that are correct and nevertheless without truth. A study that concludes that African-American students perform way below white mainstream students in reading is correct, but such a conclusion tells us very little about the material conditions with which African-American students work in the struggle against racism, educational tracking, and the systematic negation and devaluation of their histories. I would propose that the correct conclusion rests in a full understanding of the ideological elements that generate and sustain the cruel reality of racism and economic oppression. Thus an empirical study will produce conclusions without truth if it is disarticulated from the socio-cultural reality within which the subjects of the study are situated. For example, an empirical study designed to assess reading achievement of children who live in squalid conditions must factor in the reality faced by these children as accurately described by Jonathan Kozol:

> Crack-cocaine addiction and the intravenous use of heroin, which children I have met here call "the needle drug," are woven into the texture of existence in Mott Haven. Nearly 4,000 heroin

injectors, many of whom are HIV-infected, live here. Virtually every child at St. Ann's knows someone, a relative or neighbor, who has died of AIDS, and most children here know many others who are dying now of the disease. One quarter of the women of Mott Haven who are tested in obstetric wards are positive for HIV. Rates of pediatric AIDS, therefore, are high.

Depression is common among children in Mott Haven. Many cry a great deal but cannot explain exactly why.

Fear and anxiety are common. Many cannot sleep.

Asthma is the most common illness among children here. Many have to struggle to take in a good deep breath. Some mothers keep oxygen tanks, which children describe as "breathing machines," next to their children's beds.

The houses in which these children live, two thirds of which are owned by the City of New York, are often as squalid as the houses of the poorest children I have visited in rural Mississippi, but there is none of the greenness and the healing sweetness of the Mississippi countryside outside their windows, which are often barred and bolted as protection against thieves.[19]

An empirical study that neglects to incorporate in its design the cruel reality just described (and this is often the case in our supposedly classless society) will never be able to fully explain the reasons behind the poor performance of these children. Although pseudo-scientists will go to great lengths to prevent their research methodologies from being contaminated by the social ugliness described by Kozol so that they can safeguard their "objectivity" in, say, their study of underachievement of children who live in ghettos, the residents of these ghettos have little difficulty understanding the root causes of their misery, such as that described by Maria, a resident of the community.

If you weave enough bad things into the fibers of a person's life—sickness and filth, old mattresses and other junk thrown in the streets and ugly ruined things, and ruined people, a prison here, sewage there, drug dealers here, the homeless people over there, then give us the very worst schools anyone could think of, hospitals that keep you waiting for ten hours, police that don't show up when someone's dying . . . you can guess that life will not be very nice and children will not have much sense of being glad of who they are. Sometimes it feels like we have been buried six feet under their perceptions. This is what I feel they have accomplished.[20]

What this woman Maria would probably say to researchers is that we do not need another doctoral dissertation to state what is so obvious to the people sentenced to live in this form of human misery. In other words, by locking children in material conditions that are oppressive and dehumanizing we are invariably guaranteeing that they will be academically underachievers. Once the underachievement is guaranteed by these oppressive conditions, it is then very easy for research studies, such as those described in *The Bell Curve* by Richard J. Hernstein and Charles Murray, which, in the name of objectivity, are disarticulated from the political and social reality that shaped and maintain these oppressive conditions, to conclude that blacks are genetically wired to be intellectually inferior to whites. Along the same lines, an empirical study that concludes that children who engage in dinner conversation with their parents and siblings achieve higher rates of success in reading is not only academically dishonest but also misleading to the degree that it ignores the class and economic assumptions that all children are guaranteed daily dinners in the company of their parents and other siblings. What generalizations can such a study make about the 12 million children who go hungry every day in the United States? What can a study of this type say to thousands upon thousands of children who are homeless, who do not have a table and who sometimes do not have food to put on the table that they do not have? A study that makes such sweeping and distorted generalizations about the role of dinner conversations in reading achievement says little about children whose houses are without heat in the winter, houses that reach the dangerously cold conditions that led a father of four children to remark: "You just cover up ... and hope you wake up the next morning."[21] If the father really believes the study results, he will suggest to his children, after they've all made it through another freezing night alive, that they should have a conversation during dinner the next night because it will be helpful in their reading development should they be lucky enough to make it through another night alive. What dinner conversation would the Haitian immigrant, Abner Louima, have with his children after being brutally sodomized with a toilet plunger by two white policemen in a New York police precinct? Would his children's reading teacher include as part of his or her literacy development the savage acts committed by the white New York police against their father?

These questions make it clear how distorted empirical study results can be when they are disconnected from the socio-cultural reality that informs the study to begin with. In addition, such distortion feeds into the development of stereotypes that, on the one hand, blame the victims for their own social misery and, on the other hand, rationalize the genetic inferiority hypotheses that are advanced by such pseudo-scholars as Charles Murray and the former Harvard professor Richard J. Hernstein.[22] What empirical studies often neglect to point out is how easily statistics can be manipulated to take away the human face of the subjects of study through a process that not only dehumanizes but also distorts and falsifies the reality.

The inability to link research with larger critical and social issues often prevents educators not only from engaging in a general critique of the social mission of their own educational enterprise but also from acknowledging their roles as gatekeepers in reproducing the values of the dominant social order. For this reason, Grace Mitchell, a former master's degree student in the Risk and Prevention Program at the HGSE, experienced firsthand the backlash against critical theory when she insisted on questioning the program's deficit orientation model and the lack of any analysis that would link "risk" with the social, economic, political, and cultural factors that both shape and maintain oppressive conditions that generate "risk." After raising her concerns on several occasions regarding the study of "at risk" students with respect to the racist ideology within which these students exist, she was finally told in her exit interview by her site supervisor that she had been right after all and that the program does not sufficiently deal with issues of race. However, Mitchell's site practicum supervisor concluded that she was preparing something on race that she hoped would become part of the program.

After the Risk and Prevention Program resisted Mitchell's suggestions concerning race issues all year long, instead of requiring that students in the program take the Anti-Racist Multicultural Education course (which incidentally has not been offered since the spring of 1995) or the few other courses in the margin of HGSE that may critically analyze the interconnections between ideology, race, ethnicity, language, and gender, the site supervisor, a white middle-class instructor, suddenly took it upon herself to become an expert and deal with issues of race. But bell hooks is correct when she points out that many white women believe that there is "no need to hear your voice when I can talk about you better than you can speak about yourself."[23]

The lack of pedagogical space for students to ask "Who is at risk?" and "Who put these students at risk?" leads to an educational process of credentialing "experts" in risk prevention via a quick-fix intervention that leaves the inherent ideology that informs the oppressive conditions of students at risk unproblematized and unchanged.

These so-called experts in the Risk and Prevention Program, who are mostly white, middle-class individuals, are not encouraged to engage in analysis of the "at risk" reality and the ideology that informs it, which prevents them from developing a critical understanding of the interdependence between the "at risk" reality and the socio-economic and socio-cultural context that gives rise to the "at risk" reality in the first place.

The fragmentation of the study of the "at risk" reality in order to keep out the analysis of structures and mechanisms of the dominant ideology smacks of a colonial ideology whose major purpose is the systematic devaluation of the subordinated cultural expressions.

The relationship between the credentialed "experts" of "at risk" populations and the oppressed "at risk" individuals has less to do with a democratic society than with a colonial society, even though we are not allowed to call it so. If this colonial legacy remains unexamined and the "at risk" students are denied the opportunity to study and critically understand their reality, including their language, culture, gender, ethnicity, and class position, for all practical purposes the "at risk" students will continue to experience a colonial existence. Instead of becoming enslaved by the management of the "at risk" students, which enhances the economic interests of the "at risk" functionaries, educators need to reconnect with our historical past so as to understand the colonial legacy that may undermine the democratic aspirations of "at risk programs." Although Renato Constantino was writing about the colonial legacy in the Philippines, his thoughtful words are not only apropos but also illuminate our present historical juncture in education:

We see our present with as little understanding as we view our past because aspects of the past which could illuminate the present have been concealed from us. This concealment has been effected by a systemic process of mis-education characterized by

a thoroughgoing inculcation of colonial values and attitudes—
a process which could not have been so effective had we not
been denied access to the truth and to be part of our written
history. As a consequence, we have become a people without a
sense of history. We accept the present as given, bereft of historicity. Because we have so little comprehension of our past, we
have no appreciation of its meaningful interrelation with the
present.[24]

By negating history, particularly the history that engendered the
"at risk" reality, many liberals are able to safely display their pre-
sumed benevolence toward a particular subordinate cultural group
that they have labeled "at risk" without having to accept that, because of their privileged position, they are part of a social order that
created the very reality of oppression they want to study. Studying
and anthropologizing subordinated cultural groups positions many
liberals as tourists: They "become enamored and perhaps interested
in the [groups] for a time"[25] but always shield themselves from the
reality that created the conditions they want to study.

The position of many liberals in the United States is similar to
that of the leftist colonialists, who, in trying to avoid destroying their
own position of cultural privilege, found themselves caught in an
unavoidable contradiction. This contradiction surfaces often when
many liberals feel threatened by the legitimacy of the subordinate
group's struggle—a struggle that not only may not include them but
also may demand that their liberal treatment of oppression as abstract ideas be translated into concrete political action. An example
that comes to mind is an exchange that occurred during my discussion of some of these issues with graduate students at Harvard: A
middle-class white woman impatiently asked me if I was suggesting
that she give up her job. I responded that the answer was complex
but that, in some instances, giving up one's job may be necessary. I

pointed out to her that as a middle-class white Harvard graduate student she had immensely more opportunities in securing jobs than did many minority women with whom she worked in the community. Her continued occupation of a leadership position in a subordinated community meant that a minority woman would not occupy that position. I gave as an example the student Literacy Corps Tutor Training Program, which had been designed to train literacy tutors in various communities. In this program, over 86 percent of the coordinators are middle-class white women. That means that if they remain in their coordinatorship positions, minority women and men would not have the chance to occupy over 86 percent of these leadership positions. I also called to her attention the fact that minority women have infinitely less opportunity outside their racial context to compete for leadership positions.

As the discussion became a little tense, another white, middle-class student cited an episode that helped us come to a closure. She told us that a female friend of hers had given up a successful career in business to work in the community with battered mothers. Enthusiastic in her altruism, she went into a community center where she explained to one of the center staff how much more rewarding it would be to work helping people in need than it would be to work just to make money. The African-American staff member responded: "Ma'am, if you really want to help us, go back to your white folks and tell them to keep the wall of racism from crushing us." This metaphor brought home a point I was not able to make during the discussion: The issue is not to give up or not give up a job. The real issue is to understand one's privileged position in the process of helping so as not to, on the one hand, turn help into a type of missionary paternalism and, on the other hand, limit the possibilities for the creation of structures that lead to real empowerment. The metaphor also points to white teachers' responsibility to attack oppression at its very source, which is often white racist supremacy. Otherwise, the romantic desire to "empower" subordinated students leads to the insidious paternalism that provoked a Nigerian undergraduate student enrolled in a literacy tutor-training program to tell her white teacher, while they were discussing issues of oppression: "I am tired of the oppressor always reminding the oppressed of their condition."

The understanding of one's historical and privileged position requires a great deal of political clarity. However, political clarity can never be achieved if one accommodates to a position of ambiguity that usually suppresses one's ideological contradictions. This process of suppressing ideological contradiction is not just commonplace among many white liberal educators working with subordinated students; it was also a trait of the liberal colonialist who

> while he happens to dream of tomorrow, a brand-new social state in which the colonized cease to be colonized, he certainly does not conceive, on the one hand, of a deep transformation of his own situation and his personality. In that new more harmonious state, he will go on being what he is, with his language intact and his cultural traditions dominating. Through a de facto contradiction which he either does not see in himself or refuses to see, he hopes to continue being a European by divine right in a country which would no longer be Europe's chattel.[26]

This liberal colonialist contradiction is no different from that of the many white liberal educators, particularly in "risk and prevention" programs, who proselytize about empowering minorities while refusing to divest from their class-and-whiteness privilege—a privilege that is often left unexamined and unproblematized and that is often accepted as a divine right. To do otherwise is to willfully destroy one's class and color supremacy—a very difficult task, as Albert Memmi has accurately stated in his discussion of the liberal colo-

nizer: "He vaguely hopes to be part of the future young nation, but
he firmly reserves the right to remain a citizen of his native country.
... He invokes the end of colonization, but refuses to conceive that
this revolution can result in the overthrow of his situation and himself. For it is too much to ask one's own end, even if it be in order to
be reborn another."[27]

The difficulty of imagining one's own end forces many white liberal educators who want to invoke the end of oppression to embrace
a progressive methodology but not the leading ideas that may make
their own end a concrete reality. For this reason, many white educators who deal with "at risk" populations willfully adopt a benevolent
methodology but often refuse to engage the theories that inform it.
Like the white liberal "at risk" educator, "the colonist likes neither
theory nor theorists. He who knows that he is in a bad ideological or
ethical position generally boasts of being a man of action, one who
draws his lessons from experience."[28] By not theorizing their practice, the white liberal educators shield themselves from the self-criti-
cal reflection that could interrogate, among other things, how the
maintenance of their privilege invariably makes them complicit with
the dominant ideology that creates the need for them to engage in
various forms of practice in oppressed communities. Freire succinctly
understood the scapegoating of theory as a means to suffocate a more
comprehensive understanding of the reality that informs the power
asymmetries that govern our practices:

What should be contrasted with practice is not theory, which
is inseparable from it, but the nonsense of imitative thinking.
Since we can't link theory with verbalism, we can't link practice
with activism. Verbalism lacks action; activism lacks critical
reflection on action.[29]

If the "at risk" educators do not acknowledge the colonial legacy
that informs their relationship with the oppressive conditions of the

"at risk" reality, they will become at best paternalistic missionaries or, at worst, literacy and poverty pimps who make a living from the human misery with which they are in ideological complicity. It is no wonder that most of the HGSE faculty members are so easily threatened by a critical theory that challenges their complicity with the dominant ideology and the web of lies that provides them, according to Vaclav Havel, with "the repository of something 'supra-personal,' an objective [that] enables [them] to deceive their conscience and conceal their true position and their inglorious *modus vivendi*, both from the world and from themselves."[30] Paulo Freire's *Pedagogy of Freedom* courageously challenges us to break with the rigidity of a technicist training approach to education in order to embrace those fundamental knowledges that will prevent us from deceiving our conscience. In *Pedagogy of Freedom,* he brilliantly reminds us about the social order that, according to Jean-Paul Sartre, "sanctions misery, chronic hunger, ignorance, or, in general, subhumanity."[31] In essence, educators who refuse to transform the ugliness of human misery, social injustices, and inequalities, invariably become educators for domestication who, as Sartre so poignantly suggested, "will change nothing and will serve no one, but will succeed only in finding moral comfort in malaise."[32]

Donaldo Macedo
Distinguished Professor of Liberal Arts and Education
University of Massachusetts, Boston

INTRODUCTION

Prologue

Not long ago I visited a small alternative public high school in New York. It is one of the twenty or so small, mostly teacher-run high schools the sclerotic New York City Board of Education is obliged to recognize and to fund in the 1990s despite its better judgment. The board and its chancellor distrust any schools they don't control and for this reason do not leave the alternative schools to their own devices. In a system in which big is invariably viewed as better, these schools are called to account for every aspect of their operation: costs per student, number of enrolled students, their performance on standard tests, curriculum, licensure of teachers and administrators, and so on. Like most others this school was established by teachers rather than administrators, and, for this reason, its ability to survive has remained in doubt for all the years of its existence.

These alternative schools benefit from public perception that many large, board-administered high schools have failed by almost any measure: academic performance, graduation rates, college admissions, and, of course, the volume of dropouts. Most important, the secondary school behemoths fail to ignite students' passion for learning let alone demonstrate their competence by conventional testing criteria. In the typical 3,000-to-4,000-student New York City public high school, kids say "nothing is going on" except what can be provided by the occasional, unusually dedicated teacher who manages to overcome her role as a cop (keeping order is the highest priority in many of these schools) and a few energetic and entrepreneurial educators who

1

have designed and operated small programs to keep the most highly motivated from leaving the school.

The chancellor and his minions lose no opportunity to rail against these fragile experiments as cost-ineffective and irrelevant, but so far the administration has been unable to sink them because they are backed by parents and education activists and initially gained leverage on the system by raising outside foundation money to defray many start-up costs. The one I visited is among the more successful. Like many of its cohorts it was begun as a small outpost within a larger school to "contain" some of the more discontented students, many of whom would drop out unless otherwise motivated. The central administration tacitly recognizes the alternative program as a convenient way to appease an increasingly restive public and to address some of the discipline problems in many of the large, factory-like institutions.

With some 150 students, many of them Latino but also a substantial number of whites (some of whom have dropped out of the city's handful of "elite" high schools) and blacks, the five-year-old experiment has graduated some students and helped others to pass the battery of tests devised by the state to winnow the school population. These small victories resulted in its being declared a freestanding institution with its own principal. In line with the general drift, this school is organized around a "theme," although the curriculum does not suggest much specialization.

From the kids' vantage point, "Alternative High" is a magical place. Unlike many of the bigger schools, which are more day prisons than educational sites, students are not hassled by guards and assistant principals. Even more important, teachers and administrators respect and care for and about them. For many students this is the last-chance saloon: Fuck this one up and forget about a diploma, let alone college. Don't make it and it's back to the streets and maybe jail. Classes are about half the size of regular high schools, the teachers are mostly young, and several went to Ivy League schools. All work hard to engage kids in dialogue on the subject matter. (I attended classes on racial discrimination and corporate influence in contemporary higher education.) The party line of the school is antiracist and antisexist. Possessing a modest degree of autonomy, teachers use such materials as newspapers, magazines, and books rather than texts drawn from the board-prescribed reading lists. Under its "urban" program, students go out into the city to find out about neighborhood conditions, other schools, and economic issues such as joblessness. The math and science teachers are trying to integrate their subject matters and to make them concept rather than procedurally oriented. Faculty in all of the disciplines struggle to find the handles to simultaneously prepare students for the Regents Examinations, a required sorting endgame whose results have enormous bearing on whether the school will continue to exist, and what the teachers view as genuine education.

Among the teachers the name Paulo Freire is iconographic alongside the luminaries of the women's and black freedom movements, and many staff have actually read *Pedagogy of the Oppressed* or, in a general way, know something of what it contains. But the actual practice of most teachers, although relentlessly dialogic (I observed no sustained classroom lectures that followed a prescribed "lesson plan"), remained at considerable distance from Freire's own thought. At best following the dictum of the medical profession, the school manages to "first, do no harm." Now this is no small achievement in a system that routinely inflicts incredible damage on kids, and not only on working class kids from racial, sexual, or gendered strata. Alternative High's students displayed veritable exhilaration at being there. They feel safe. And I suspect that its greatest accomplishment has been to establish relations of trust among the slender corps of administrators, teachers, and students. What is truly innovative about the school is its fealty to one of Freire's prerequisites: respect for kids and what they already know. But as to education, it has a long way to go. In fact, in concert with many liberal and radical educators, some teachers have interpreted liberatory education to chiefly mean instilling humanistic values in a nonrepressive way. The school seems to be a massive values clarification exercise.

These are dark times for educational innovation and its protagonists. In schools and universities "reactionaries" (as Paulo Freire calls them) have all but overwhelmed the "progressives." Their agenda to construe the very concept of education as training dominates schooling in public universities and is steadily gaining ground in private institutions as well. During the last decade, schools that insisted on their difference committed an unholy violation of the new common sense that the highest mission and overriding purpose of schooling was to prepare students, at different levels, to take their places in the corporate order. The banking or transmission theory of school knowledge, which Freire identified more than thirty years ago as the culprit standing in the way of critical consciousness, has returned with a vengeance. Once widely scorned by educators from diverse educational philosophies as a flagrant violation of the democratic educational mission, it has been thrust to the fore of nearly all official pedagogy. According to this view, students are "objects" into which teachers pour prescribed knowledge, in the first place mathematics and rote science. Where once liberal, let alone radical, educators insisted that education be at the core an activity of self-exploration in which, through intellectual and affective encounters, the student attempts to discover her own subjectivity, now nearly all learning space is occupied by an elaborate testing apparatus that measures the student's "progress" in ingesting externally imposed curriculae and, more insidiously, provides a sorting device to reproduce the inequalities inherent in the capitalist market system. In effect, when not viewed as a bundle of uncontrollable animal urges, intellectually the image of the learner has reverted to Locke's infamous tabula rasa. In turn, the teacher becomes the instrument of approved intellectual and moral culture, charged with the task of expunging destructive impulses and fueling the empty mental tank. The student must be permitted no autonomy lest the evil spirits that lurk in everyday life regain lost ground.

These perspectives have reached across the ideological spectrum. In various degrees academics and school authorities have embraced the new mantra that the student and radical movements of the 1960s and 1970s, which, internationally, forced educational reforms such as open classrooms, student-generated curricula, and black, women's, and ethnic studies programs and introduced into the canon of many human sciences the works of Marx and the Marxists, Derrida, Foucault, Deleuze, and French feminists, were intellectual terrorism. Especially after the fall of the Berlin Wall, some intellectuals discovered their own liberalism and others kept drifting rightward. In the United States a range of erstwhile leftists—even those who had perpetrated what philosopher Sidney Hook once described as elements of academic "anarchy"—began to accept chairs and grant money from leading conservative institutions, such as the Olin Foundation, to enjoy the company of the enemies of critical learning. For many the radicalism of the 1960s and 1970s turned out to be a horror show of "political correctness," a menace to the integrity of the academic enterprise, the highest value of which was dispassionate, disinterested scientific investigation. The radicals became "ideologues" because they took sides; the others were "scholars" because their side was the liberal academy with its panoply of discipline-based departments, professional associations, and literatures. For them, what America and the world needed was schooling that obliged students to keep their collective noses to the grindstone in order to imbibe the best that had been thought and said. The highest curricular value was the dissemination of the "Great Traditions" of what they called Western Civilization.

For example, in elementary schools the reactionaries have recently begun to eliminate "recess," the small opportunity kids still enjoy to play during the school day. For the mavens of authoritarian education, such frivolous pursuits must be replaced by the industrial model, which in former periods was reserved for secondary school. In this age of the subsumption of the human spirit under the imperatives of alienated work without end, society has lost its tolerance for even kid pleasures, and school authorities have, sometimes enthusiastically, subordinated themselves to business by imaging schools in the modalities of the factory or the large corporate office. Even where the values of business civilization are not (yet) openly trumpeted by administrators, their tolerance for changes suggested by the new social movements has worn thin.

In this environment *Pedagogy of Freedom*—Paulo Freire's last book—is a utopian text. Its utopianism consists of the wild—and seemingly anachronistic—idea that among other things education is "that specifically human act of intervening in the world." "When I speak of intervention," Freire says, "I refer both to the aspiration for radical changes in society in such areas as economics, human relations, property, the right to employment, to land, to education, and to health, to the reactionary position whose aim is to immobilize history and maintain an unjust socio-economic and cultural order." As he utters these words Freire almost hears an interlocutor's sigh: "Yeah, yeah, yeah, we've heard all that before, but what makes you think any change is possible in the era of unfettered global capitalism when the forces of progressive reason have yielded even the territory of the imagination to its adversaries?" Or what amounts to the same thing: "Poor people cannot afford idle dreams, professor. Get real. What kids need is job readiness." In fact, he acknowledges that many have succumbed to fatalism, pessimism, and the program of "neoliberalism," the doctrine according to which we have no choice but to adapt both our hopes and our abilities to the new global market. In short, this book contains no dewy-eyed, ingenuous optimism. Freire is simply stating what genuine education is and what the role of the teacher and learner is in the process. He renounces the prevailing pretense of the teacher's "neutrality" or "impartiality." Indeed, he argues that few teachers can sustain this claim in a time when schooling is undergoing unprecedented regimentation.

What then is the basis of hope for genuine education as Freire defines it when the corporate CEO is a culture hero, when techno-scientific training has been elevated to the pedagogic norm, and when the remnants of the once vast army of educational liberals have retreated to the sacred texts? How can anyone fail to realize that the language of radical change, let alone the chance of its realization, toppled with the Berlin Wall a decade ago and now belongs with other relics of that bygone era? Freire answers that he has an "obstinate fascination with everything that has to do with men and women." So for him it is never a question of demonstrating that education is likely, only that it is possible. Freire aligns himself with those who still dream and keep alive hope for a world without exploitation, inequality, and cultural enslavement. But, unlike neoliberals and some leftists, his conviction is not borne out by some "scientific" assessment of the current situation. Instead, Freire's belief in the emancipation of men and women is rooted in an "existential" commitment to an ethical ideal rather than to historical inevitability. In our period of crass opportunism and crushed aspirations, this book is a beacon for those with whom he is affiliated: "the wretched of the earth, the excluded." But unlike those who, sixty years earlier, despaired for a better world at the moment of fascism's rise and could offer only the "Great Refusal," a negative prescription to resist the totalitarian machine, Freire finds affirmation in the achievements of countless teachers and students who have defied the new authoritarian machine to conquer illiteracy, to assert their "critical curiosity" to intervene. Careful to distinguish educational activity from revolutionary transformation, he nevertheless defends it as a significant break from the status quo and a necessary step on the road to a different future than that proposed by the reactionaries. Freire seems to suggest that a radical futurity depends upon the work of radical educators today.

Since the English translation thirty years ago of his widely read book *Pedagogy of the Oppressed*, Freire's work has suffered the misreadings of well-meaning educators who have interpreted his work as a "brilliant methodology," a kind of manual for teachers who would bring out the best in their otherwise indifferent students. Such characterizations are undoubtedly fed by the common identification of pedagogy merely with compassionate teaching: What is taught is unproblematic; the only issue is how to teach on the basis of caring. As a certified possessor of legitimate knowledge, the teacher's authority is fundamentally always already established, and the student's position as a consumer of knowledge is equally unquestioned. So, many read Freire's dialogic pedagogy as a tool for student motivation and cannot recognize that for him dialogue is a content whose goal is social as much as individual change. In Freire's educational philosophy the first principle is that the conventional distinction between teacher as expert and learner as an empty bio-physiological shell is questioned. Education takes place when there are two learners who occupy somewhat different spaces in an ongoing dialogue. But both participants bring knowledge to the relationship, and one of the objects of the pedagogic process is to explore what each knows and what they can teach each other. A second object is to foster reflection on the self as actor in the world in consequence of knowing.

Against the prevailing wisdom, Freire rejects the idea of teacher as transmitter of received knowledge. But he also spurns the degraded idea that the teacher is chiefly a "facilitator" of commonsense wisdom and of values clarification. Alternatively he argues for the teacher as an intellectual who, like the student, is engaged preeminently in producing knowledge. But to create new knowledge, the teacher and the student come to the learning situation as possessors of past knowledge, albeit of different sorts. The student arrives with his life experience and his previous schooling in hand. An important moment in the learning situation is when the student critically evaluates what she knows and not only for the purpose of overcoming these knowledges. Consistent with the Hegelianism inherent in his own practice, Freire wants to preserve as well as transform what the student knows, to make it available in the process of knowledge production. Reflection is an occasion for the student's intervention in examining and changing life.

The teacher brings to the relationship several different "contents." As opposed to some of his most fervent supporters, Freire does not hesitate to put his own intellectual sources on the table, in the first place Marx, who grasped the historicity of all social and economic systems and declared that the producers, including the producers of knowledge, were capable of making their own history. (In *Pedagogy of Freedom* Freire carefully distances himself from the "end of history" crowd, placing them in the neoliberal camp.) Then with the radicals within psychology who, like Erich Fromm, explored the burning question of why people fear the freedom that comes with knowing/acting in the world, Freire identifies what may be termed the internalized authority of the master as the source of the reproduction of oppression and an obstacle to the formation of the "subject."

But Freire does not reify the bearers of progressive ideologies. To the insight that people are often invested in their own oppression and resist change because, in addition to taking on the worldview of the master, they recoil at taking risk, he adds that the practice of some who would assist in the project of human emancipation belies their intentions. It is not only the Right that proposes to bring predigested enlightenment to the masses from on high. Although in the present book his critique of authoritarian leftism is not explicit—he aims most of his fire at those within Brazil and elsewhere who, in cynical despair, have turned from the radical project—his disdain for change *from above* regardless from what end of the political spectrum is crystal clear. Freire insists on the ineluctable connection between democracy from below—radical democracy—and human liberation. No doubt this worldview will come as a suprise to many who have consulted only his early work, which is still influenced by political and intellectual vanguardism. Since Freire's later position is that radical futurity is indeterminate and he has taken into account the pitfalls of the actual experience of revolutionary regimes, including some with which he collaborated, there is no question of working from a series of received truths.

Between his early and late writings the third source, the phenomenological and existential philosophy of writers like Jean-Paul Sartre, remains, perhaps, the most controversial. Controversial to those who seek to root hope in the dialectic of history, who would, despite all, refuse Freire problematizing specific historical agents. Perhaps his shift from certainty to indeterminacy may be ascribed to the circumstances of his own political experience, to the failures as much as the successes of his own work and of his observations of others' attempts to change the world by applying formulaic Marxism to concrete conditions. In this and his more recent writings, Freire's commitments are rooted neither in the inevitability of historical transformation nor in the leadership of revolutionary vanguards. Although Freire reminds us the teacher is an actor on the social and political stage, the educator's task is to encourage human agency, not mold it in the manner of Pygmalion. What propels his unceasing efforts to marshal the spirit of "rebelliousness" is ethical rather than scientific conviction, the belief that, having taken sides, the teacher is obliged to struggle with only hope of realizing only his own ideals.

Freire remains a humanist in two ways. His discourse is anthropocentric despite recent ecological and paleobiological evidence that the link between some mammals and humans is closer at virtually all developmental levels than was previously believed. For Freire, humans alone have critical capacities, a judgment that is certainly arguable. That Freire chooses to assert this faith should be seen in the context of the battles he waged against those who would deny to education its critical function. And his is a humanist ethic insofar as class societies retard the development of the capacities of people to take control of their own destinies. Holding that education is a form of "ideology," Freire believes the teacher takes sides between those who have appropriated the wealth, the land, and the knowledge of the social and cultural system and the dispossessed. Freire judges current social and political arrangements by the criterion of whether they have taken steps to amelioriate, much less reverse, the long tradition of authoritarian societies to exclude substantial portions of their populations from participation in economic, social, and cultural life and whether they further or retard humanity's project of self-fulfillment. Finding that in his native land, Brazil, neoliberalism has done little to change the conditions of life for ordinary people, he joined the opposition Workers Party and became its first secretary of education when it took power in the city of São Paulo in 1991.

The book before you is, in part, a reflection on this experience. Even though there is little in the way of a memoir of his two years as a government official, Freire tacitly admits the huge frustration of trying to undertake school reform within a system that, in a large measure, is deprived and in turn deprives students of the most elementary tools of education: adequate funds with which to assure a full school day, materials, and safe facilities; a commitment to kids as "subjects"; and teachers who are aware that theirs is a political as well as intellectual project. That in the face of bitter disappointments Freire sees fit to reiterate the principle of hope that underlies his life's work is altogether remarkable. But there is also a powerfully prescriptive side to this text. Even more than its predecessors, this work delineates what a pedagogy of freedom entails.

Although written from Brazil in the late 1990s when the early promise of renewal after the passing of the military dictatorship has been betrayed by, among others, some of the very intellectuals who hastened the dictatorship's demise, this book is more than an inspiring testament by an old warrior. It is nothing less than an invocation to seekers after an alternative to repressive education to renew the struggle for emancipatory education. First, it advocates a "rigorous ethical grounding" in the teacher's determination to combat "racial, sexual, and class discrimination." Second, it explains the concept that education is open-ended "scientific formation" because people are conditioned but not determined by their circumstances. What does Freire mean by science in this regard? Surely not the humdrum formulaic techniques characteristic of most of our school pedagogies. Freire calls for the learner's "critical reflection" on the social, economic, and cultural conditions within which education occurs; learning begins with taking the self as the first—but not the last—object of knowledge. Education does not stop with dialogue. The teacher is obliged to engage in "exposition and explanation" of those economic and social conditions that bear on the educational process and to expose students to many of the sacred texts without which education degenerates into opinion. But the self is for him a social concept, one that entails the whole world.

Finally, since teachers are learners as well, they are not figures independent of the social process. Teachers are chronically underpaid, subject to onerous working and living conditions, and, I would add, often poorly educated. Part of Freire's ethical idea is the absolute necessity of teachers' self-defense of their own dignity, a struggle that includes their "right" to academic freedom, to have autonomy in the construction of the curriculum and of the pedagogic process. In this respect he invokes two separate rationales. Dedicated to the unity of theory and practice, teachers can hardly make credible the link between education and action if they themselves are not so engaged. But teachers cannot be effective when they remain in the thrall of an exploitative school system that robs them of their own voice.

These principles, enunciated on the heels of Freire's more recent *urban* frame of reference, as contrasted with his earlier focus on rural communities, especially in Brazil and Africa, should make his ideas more resonant to educators and activists in more advanced industrial societies. São Paulo, a city of more than 12 million inhabitants, exhibits the full range of social, cultural, and economic conditions found in any of the world's large cities: Mexico City, New York, London, Los Angeles, Atlanta. It is a place of wealth, basic industry, and grinding poverty born of the rural crisis and chronic unemployment. Like elsewhere its middle class is embattled under the weight of multiple uncertainties wrought by globalization and political turmoil. Freire's special concern has not diminished for the "ragpickers" and the "wretched" who live in favellas—those vast stretches of impoverished communities composed of the unemployed and underemployed living in conditions of makeshift tin and cardboard dwellings in São Paulo and many other major cities of Latin America. Yet he takes pains to speak of his pedagogy as "universal." In this respect we may take *Pedagogy of Freedom* as the basis of what Nietzsche calls "new principles of evaluation," where the term "evaluation" indicates not a fixed set of criteria from which to make superficial measurements of social policies but a series of concepts by which to forge a new educational process.

Among these concepts is the open, full-throated declaration that the idea of the educator as a disinterested purveyor of "objective" knowledge, the incontrovertible "facts" that form the foundation of dominant values, is itself a form of ideological discourse. If Freire does not go so far as to declare that there are no "facts" for which power is the underlying legitimation or that every statement about the world is an interpretation, he does criticize the positive doctrine according to which the "givens" of the taken-for-granted world must be viewed as the immutable starting points of learning and its companion, the privileged position of "methodology" for learning. How to square such principles with his oft -repeated dedication to "scientific" formation? Freire's notion of science is difficult for Anglo-American readers because it seems to grate against conventional conceptions of science's social "neutrality" and value freedom.

Freire stands firmly in the tradition for which the definition of science is critical and not positivistic. Educational formation becomes "scientific" when the learner grasps the link between theory and practice through a process whose assumption is that the individual is, in every respect, "unfinished." The accomplishment of critical consciousness consists in the first place in the learner's capacity to situate herself in her own historicity, for example, to grasp the class, race, and sexual aspects of education and social formation and to understand the complexity of the relations that have produced this situation. Such an accomplishment entails a critical examination of received wisdom, not as a storehouse of eternal truths but as itself situated in its own historicity. Implicit in this process is the concept that each of us embodies universality but that it does not necessarily dominate us. Thus, the active knower, not the mind as a repository of "information," is the goal of education.

The widespread acquiescence by students and their families to the rigors of techno-scientific training may be explained by the artificial imposition of a new scarcity regime in the global capitalist system.

As good jobs disappear and are replaced by temporary, contingent, and part-time work, competition among prospective workers intensifies. The school responds by making testing the object of teaching and, in the bargain, robs teachers of their intellectual autonomy, not to say intellectual function. As education is supressed and replaced by training, students learn that critical consciousness is dangerous to the end of techno-scientific formation because it may jeopardize their chance for a job, let alone a career. Critical educators may be admired but dismissed as propagandists; fearing marginalization some teachers may try to reconcile their views with those of neoliberalism by arguing that Freire's "method" might produce more creative employees for entrepreneurial corporations or lift some poor and working class students from inexorable subordination to individual social mobility. After all, even the most conservative cultures require self-justification by picking out a few subalterns to promote as emblems of the system's flexibility.

But Freire's admirers should remember that in 1964 the military regime sent him into exile for his ideas, that he was forced to roam the world for the next twenty-five years before it was possible to return home. The authoritarians in Western societies and the new liberal democracies of Latin America may or may not resort to exile or imprisonment to silence critical educators. But the will to power almost inevitably requires that subversive ideas such as these be silenced or so mutated that only the husk is recognized as legitimate. Even in ostensibly democratic societies, those who would bring dialogic and critical practices into classrooms risk marginalization.

Under these circumstances critical educators have no alternative but to organize through unions, study groups, institutes, schools, and other sites to actively propagate these new principles of educational evaluation. Needless to say in this conservative era, the task is daunting. One of the most important uncompleted tasks before those who would preserve Freire's legacy is to elaborate an educational philosophy and strategy for economically developed societies and for an increasingly economically and culturally interdependent world. Perhaps the most significant intervention would be in the raging educational debates of our time. In the current climate liberal educators are hopelessly outgunned—intellectually as well as politically and financially. They have retreated from their humanistic positions, conceding the need for vocationalization of the lion's share of the school curriculum in working-class communities. Even educators in elite schools are constrained to hold the line against corporate incursions. In major private universities there is little resistance to the inducements of conservative, corporate foundations who have offered chairs in virtually every field if the institution will accept or consider the foundation's nominee seriously. None has evaluated the effect on the nature and scope of scientific inquiry of proliferating agreements between researchers and bio-technology and information corporations to focus research on applications that lead directly to product development. Nor are the celebrants of the Human Genome Project, the largest U.S. government-supported science program, visibly fazed by the enormous implications of the program: vast possibilities for surveillance of ordinary citizens; a virulent revival of eugenically oriented education; and the foundation for bio-engineering programs, military applications, and so on.

Today many defend the humanities and arts curricula as valuable adjuncts to business and occupationally oriented programs at the secondary as well as higher educational levels. They argue that the well-rounded accountant should know something about opera, that the financial counselor or broker needs to write a literate memo or report, that managers perform their jobs better if they understand human psychology. As humanities and social science majors continue to drop or stagnate at undergraduate institutions, the professoriat is under intense market pressure to justify its existence. Schools measure their hipness by the number of computers they can place in the classroom, whether they have a viable internship program with prospective employers, and, in universities and colleges, whether they value their "development" (grant-seeking) activities above all others in the academic "enterprise."

The critical educational project faces an uphill battle if it argues that "critical consciousness," as opposed to critical thinking as a "skill," should be the motive force of education and that its process as well as its outcome is a generation of intervenors in the social and political life of this planet. Not only would this program encounter opposition from the reactionaries whose agenda is, more and more, frankly to subsume schools to corporate requirements but also from liberals and progressives who cling to the neutrality of education just as scientists insist on their inculpability regarding the uses of their discoveries and inventions. Critical education must expose the new alliance of many in the liberal intelligentsia with the dominant culture without fixing moral blame. Although Freire calls on teachers and others to take sides on ethical precepts, I have detected not a sentence of guiltmongering or accusation against intellectuals who have responded to the ideological and political assaults against education by bending their principles to the program of the Right. In *Pedagogy of Freedom* he implies an explanation for this capitulation. Their political spirit has been degraded by their inability to offer resistance and alternatives, to act in their own behalf when working conditions deteriorate and salaries are under attack. Freire points to collective solutions as well as individual responsibility for intervening. His critique is political and not moral.

While a bold critique of the Right is urgent, a critical educational movement would be obliged to undertake a dialogue with the teachers in places like Alternative U as well as progressives in educational programs in communities, labor unions, and mainstream schools. Although their hearts are pure and their motivation impeccable, many in the alternative school movement have settled for providing a safe haven for troubled students and in the bargain have, often unwittingly, adopted anti-intellectualism as armor against those who would destroy even this basic gain. Teachers in mainstream schools feel embattled and are grateful to insert a bit of critical learning within the confines of the classroom. And trade union educators, especially in the United States, have narrowed their horizon to encompass the bare bones of union contract administration and a little legislative and political education. But "consciensization," Freire's perennial phrase for critical self-consciousness, requires the teacher be able to undertake "exposition and explanation" as elements of the dialogue. In order to facilitate the critical faculties and the intellectual development, the teacher must offer theoretical perspectives as well as a loving environment for student self-expression without conveying the message that these are party line standpoints and texts are chosen only to buttress them. For as every good teacher knows, if students perceive that the teacher is pro-student there are few limits to possible manipulation. At Alternative High students were well aware of the party line, and it was a regular butt of their bitterly ironic humor.

Therefore, the teacher must take the role of the "other" to present the most reasonable and articulate version of opposing views, must assign persuasive conservative texts, and must treat them seriously by means of exposition as well as refutation. In this process the teacher is aware that well-wrought hegemonic ideas may persuade better than her own counterhegemonies. The risk of critical education is that if schools are constructed as genuine public spheres outcomes are not guaranteed.

That Freire's last testament should focus on the question of freedom may, at first glance, confuse some readers. For isn't "freedom" the favorite slogan of the antiradicals? What, indeed, does freedom mean, especially in education? On the plane of politics Freire clearly takes his stand with those who would create social and economic arrangements that, while dedicated to more equality, go beyond the urgent task of eliminating poverty, hunger, and disease. The good life is not merely having a job, enough to eat, and decent shelter. Authoritarians have, from time to time, been able to deliver this much, at least for limited periods. Freire holds that a humanized society requires cultural freedom, the ability of the individual to choose values and rules of conduct that violate conventional social norms, and, in political and civil society, requires the full participation of *all* of its inhabitants in every aspect of public life. But people cannot raise themselves to bid for power unless their curiousity has been aroused to ask the hard questions: "why" as well as "what." For Freire, then, "the foundation stone of the whole [educational] process is human curiosity. This is what makes me question, know, act, ask again, recognize." A learner who has reached this point is ready to demand power, which, after all, is the object of any pedagogy of freedom.

Stanley Aronowitz
Distinguished Professor of Sociology and Cultural Studies
Graduate School of City University of New York

ONE

INTRODUCTORY REFLECTIONS

Two subjects occupy me in the writing of this text. The question of what forms education and becoming a teacher, and a reflection on educative practice from a progressive point of view. By "progressive" I mean a point of view that favors the autonomy of the students. This theme of autonomy incorporates the analysis of various types of knowledge that I find to be fundamental to educational practice. And, if there are other types of knowledge that I have left out or whose importance I have not appreciated, I hope the critical reader will be able to add them to the list.

To those who may read this book, I ought at the outset to make clear that since this theme is a permanent preoccupation of mine as a teacher, various aspects of it, discussed here, will have been discussed in my earlier books. I do not believe, however, that the fact that I touch on these problems from one book to another is wearisome to the reader, especially when they are taken up again in a nonrepetitive way. In my own case, taking up a theme again and again has to do principally with the oral status of my written word. It also has to do with the relevance of the theme of which I speak to the array of objects in which I invest my curiosity. And it has to do with the relationship that certain things have with other things, as they emerge during the course of my reflection. It is in this sense, for example, that I once again touch on the question of the unfinishedness of the human person, the question of our insertion into a permanent process of searching. In this context I explore again the problem of ingenuous and critical curiosity and the epistemological status of curiosity. It is also in this sense that I insist once again that education (or "formation" as I sometimes call it) is much more than a question of training a student to be dexterous or competent. I also may as well mention my almost obstinate fascination with everything that has to do with men and women. I keep returning to this topic, and each time I do so, it is as if I am coming to it enchanted for the first time. Finally, I cannot avoid a permanently critical attitude toward what I consider to be the scourge of neoliberalism, with its cynical fatalism and its inflexible negation of the right to dream differently, to dream of utopia.

My abhorrence of neoliberalism helps to explain my legitimate anger when I speak of the injustices to which the ragpickers among humanity are condemned. It also explains my total lack of interest in any pretension of impartiality. I am not impartial or objective; not a fixed observer of facts and happenings. I never was able to be an adherent of the traits that falsely claim impartiality or objectivity. That did not prevent me, however, from holding always a rigorously ethical position. Whoever really observes, does so from a given point of view. And this does not necessarily mean that the observer's position is erroneous. It is an error when one becomes dogmatic about one's point of view and ignores the fact that, even if one is certain about his or her point of view, it does not mean that one's position is always ethically grounded.

My point of view is that of the "wretched of the earth," of the excluded. I do not accept, however, under any circumstances, acts of terrorism in support of this point of view. Such acts result in the death of the innocent and the spread of an insecurity that affects everyone. Terrorism is the negation of what I call a universal human ethic. I am on the side of the Arabs in their struggle for their rights, but I cannot accept the acts of terrorism perpetrated in Munich and elsewhere in favor of those rights.

I would like to underline what I consider to be for teachers our ethical responsibility in the exercise of our profession. And this applies also to those who are, at present, in the course of preparing themselves to be teachers. This small book is permeated by and cut across with the total sense of the nature of ethics that is inherent in all forms of educational practice, especially as this practice pertains to the preparation of teachers. Teacher preparation should never be reduced to a form of training. Rather, teacher preparation should go beyond the technical preparation of teachers and be rooted in the ethical formation both of selves and of history. But it is important to be clear that I am speaking not about a restricted kind of ethics that shows obedience only to the law of profit. Namely, the ethics of the market. It seems that there is now a global tendency to accept the crucial implications of the New World Order as natural and inevitable. One of the speakers at a recent international meeting of nongovernmental organizations (NGOs) reports of hearing an opinion, frequently bandied about in the first world, that third world children suffering from acute diarrhea ought not be saved because we would only prolong lives destined for misery and suffering.[1] Obviously, I am not speaking of that kind of ethics. On the contrary, I am speaking of a universal human ethic, an ethic that is not afraid to condemn the kind of ideological discourse I have just cited. Not afraid to condemn the exploitation of labor and the manipulation that makes a rumor into truth and truth into a mere rumor. To condemn the fabrication of illusions, in which the unprepared become hopelessly trapped and the weak and the defenseless are destroyed. To condemn making promises when one has no intention of keeping one's word, which causes lying to become an almost necessary way of life. To condemn the calumny of character assassination simply for the joy of it and the fragmentation of the utopia of human solidarity. The ethic of which I speak is that which feels itself betrayed and neglected by the hypocritical perversion of an elitist purity, an ethic affronted by racial, sexual, and class discrimination. For the sake of this ethic, which is inseparable from educative practice, we should struggle, whether our work is with children, youth, or adults.

The best way to struggle for this ethic is to live it in our educative practice, in our relations with our students, in the way we deal with the contents of what we teach, and in the way we quote from authors—both those we agree with and those we do not. We cannot criticize an author unless we actually know his or her work. To base a criticism merely on ideas about the author gleaned from the book cover is an insult.

I may not agree with a given pedagogical theory of this or that author, and, of course, I ought to make my students aware of the disagreement. But what I cannot do in my criticism is lie to them. The education of the teacher should be so ethically grounded that any gap between professional and ethical formation is to be deplored. We should devote ourselves humbly but perseveringly to our profession in all its aspects: scientific formation, ethical rectitude, respect for others, coherence, a capacity to live with and learn from what is different, and an ability to relate to others without letting our ill-humor or our antipathy get in the way of our balanced judgment of the facts.

It is not only of interest to students but also extremely important to students to perceive the differences that exist among teachers over the comprehension, interpretation, and appreciation, sometimes widely differing, of problems and questions that arise in the day-to-day learning situations in the classroom. It is also fundamental that they perceive the respect and loyalty with which a teacher may analyze or criticize the position of a colleague.

From time to time, in the course of this book, I will be returning to this theme because I am absolutely convinced of the ethical nature of educative practice in so far as it is a specifically human activity. Also given the fact that every country on the planet is becoming more and more suffocated by the ethics of the market, it seems to me that whatever we do to promote a universal human ethic is very little compared with what needs to be done. We can only consider ourselves to be the subjects of our decisions, our searching, our capacity to choose—that is, as historical subjects, as people capable of transforming our world—if we are grounded ethically. In this sense, the possibility of transgressing our ethical foundation exists and is a choice. But it is not a virtue, and we cannot accept it.

It is not possible for the ethical subject to live without being permanently exposed to the risk or even the choice of transgression. One of the biggest difficulties about this ethical grounding is that we have to do everything in our power to sustain a universal human ethic without at the same time falling into a hypocritical moralism. Simultaneously, it is part of our struggle for such an ethic to refuse, with dignity, the defense of a human ethic that is quite obviously only a mask for pharisaical moralism. I have never indulged in distortion or negation as far as this ethic is concerned.

When I speak of a universal human ethic, however, I am speaking of something absolutely indispensable for human living and human social intercourse. In making this statement, I am aware of the critical voices of those who, because they do not know where I am coming from, consider me ingenuous and idealistic. In truth, I speak of a universal human ethic in the same way I speak of humanity's ontological vocation, which calls us out of and beyond ourselves. Or as I speak of our being as something constructed socially and historically and not there simply a priori. A being born in the womb of history but in the process of coming to be bears in itself some fundamental archetypes without which it would be impossible to recognize our human presence in the world as something singular and original. In other words, our being in the world is far more than just "being." It is a "presence," a "presence" that is relational to the world and to others. A "presence" that, in recognizing another presence as "not I," recognizes its own self. A "presence" that can reflect upon itself, that knows itself as presence, that can intervene, can transform, can speak of what it does, but that can also take stock of, compare, evaluate, give value to, decide, break with, and dream. It is in the area of decision, evaluation, freedom, breaking with, option, that the ethical necessity imposes itself. In this sense, ethical grounding is inevitable, although its transgression is also possible. And transgression occurs. It cannot be considered a value even though it is the fruit of choice. It is not, in other words, a virtue.

In truth, it would be incomprehensible if the awareness that I have of my presence in the world were not, simultaneously, a sign of the impossibility of my absence from the construction of that presence. Insofar as I am a conscious presence in the world, I cannot hope to escape my ethical responsibility for my action in the world. If I am a pure product of genetic, cultural, or class determination, I have no responsibility for my action in the world and, therefore, it is not possible for me to speak of ethics. Of course, this assumption of responsibility does not mean that we are not conditioned genetically, culturally, and socially. It means that we know ourselves to be *conditioned* but not *determined*. It means recognizing that History is time filled with possibility and not inexorably determined—that the future is *problematic* and not already decided, fatalistically.

I should stress also that this book is about hope and optimism, but not about false optimism or vain hope. Of course, people will say—including some on the left for whom the future has lost its problematic essence and is now no more than a given—that this optimism and hope of mine are nothing but the daydream of an inveterate dreamer.

I am not angry with people who think pessimistically. But I am sad because for me they have lost their place in history.

There is a lot of fatalism around us. An immobilizing ideology of fatalism, with its flighty postmodern pragmatism, which insists that we can do nothing to change the march of social-historical and cultural reality because that is how the world is anyway. The most dominant contemporary version of such fatalism is neoliberalism. With it, we are led to believe that mass unemployment on a global scale is an end-of-the-century inevitability. From the standpoint of such an ideology, only one road is open as far as educative practice is concerned: adapt the student to what is inevitable, to what cannot be changed. In this view, what is essential is technical training, so that the student can adapt and, therefore, survive. This book, which I now offer to those who are interested in this theme, is a decisive NO to an ideology that humiliates and denies our humanity.

Lastly, let me say what this book asks and hopes of you: That you give yourself to it critically and with ever-expanding curiosity.

THERE IS NO TEACHING
WITHOUT LEARNING

Although my main interest in this book is to look at the kind of knowledge that is indispensable to educators who consider themselves to be critical progressives, such knowledge may be indispensable to educators who regard themselves as conservatives. I refer here to the kind of knowledge that belongs inherently to educative practice itself, whatever the political persuasion of the educator.

As the chapters unfold, the reader can make up his or her own mind as to whether the knowledge I discuss is part of progressive or conservative educative practice or is an intrinsic requirement of educational practice itself, independent of political or ideological coloring. In previous writings, I have referred to various aspects of this kind of knowledge, though not in any systematic way. Even so, it seems to me legitimate to continue this kind of reflection in the context of teacher preparation and in critical educational practice.

Let us take, for example, the practice of cooking. Cooking presupposes certain kinds of knowledge regarding the use of the cooking stove. How to light it. How to turn the heat up and down. How to deal with the possibility of fire. How to balance the ingredients in a harmonious and pleasing synthesis. With practice newcomers to the kitchen will confirm some of the things they already know, correct others that they do not know so well, and gradually open up the way to become cooks. The practice of sailing requires some fundamental knowledge about the control of the boat, the parts of which it is made, and the function of each of them. It requires, in addition, a capacity to measure and interpret the strength and direction of the winds, to gauge the interaction between the wind and sail, and to position the sails themselves. It requires, too, some knowledge of the motor and the relationship between it and the sails. And, in the practice of sailing, all these kinds of knowledge are either confirmed, modified, or amplified.

Critical reflection on practice is a requirement of the relationship between theory and practice. Otherwise theory becomes simply "blah, blah, blah," and practice, pure activism.

But let me return to what interests me here. I want to focus on and discuss some of the kinds of knowledge that are fundamental to what I call critical (or progressive) educative practice and that, for that reason, ought to be considered essential in the teacher preparation program. Essential in their comprehension and lucid clarity. The very first of these types of knowledge, indispensable from the beginning to the teacher (that is, to the teacher who considers him- or herself to be an agent in the production of knowledge), is that to teach is not *to transfer knowledge* but to create the possibilities for the production or construction of knowledge.

If, during the time of my education, which in any case should be ongoing, I begin believing that my teacher is the "subject" in relation to whom I consider myself to be the "object" (if, in other words, he/ she is the subject who forms me, and I, the object shaped by him or her), then I put myself in the passive role of one who receives quantities of accumulated knowledge, transferred to me by a "subject" who "knows." Living and understanding my educational process in this way, I, as "object," will become in my turn a false subject, responsible for the reproduction of further objects. It is essential therefore, from the very beginning of the process, that the following principle be clear: namely, that although the teachers or the students are not the same, the person in charge of education is being formed or re-formed as he/she teaches, and the person who is being taught forms him/herself in this process. In this sense teaching is not about transferring knowledge or contents. Nor is it an act whereby a creator-subject gives shape, style, or soul to an indecisive and complacent body. There is, in fact, no teaching without learning. One requires the other. And the subject of each, despite their obvious differences, cannot be educated to the status of object. Whoever teaches learns in the act of teaching, and whoever learns teaches in the act of learning. From the grammatical point of view, the verb to teach is a "transitive-relative" verb, that is, a verb that requires a direct object (something) and an indirect object (to someone). In this sense, to teach is teaching something to someone. But to teach is much more than a transitive-relative verb. And this is clear not only from the context of democratic thought in which I place myself but also from an essentially metaphysical point of view in which my comprehension of the cognitive process is grounded. In other words, simply "to teach" is not possible in the context of human historical unfinishedness. Socially and historically, women and men discovered that it was the process of learning that made (and makes) teaching possible. Learning in social contexts through the ages, people discovered that it was possible to develop ways, paths, and methods of teaching. To learn, then, logically precedes to teach. In other words, to teach is part of the very fabric of learning. This is true to such an extent that I do not hesitate to say that there is no valid teaching from which there does not emerge something learned and through which the learner does not become capable of recreating and remaking what has been thought. In essence, teaching that does not emerge from the experience of learning cannot be learned by anyone.

When we live our lives with the authenticity demanded by the practice of teaching that is also learning and learning that is also teaching, we are participating in a total experience that is simultaneously directive, political, ideological, gnostic, pedagogical, aesthetic, and ethical. In this experience the beautiful, the decent, and the serious form a circle with hands joined.

At times, in moments of silence when I seem to be lost, floating, almost disconnected, I reflect on the way that women and men are and have become "programmed for learning," in the words of François Jacob.[1] In other words, the process of learning, through which historically we have discovered that teaching is a task not only inherent to the learning process but is also characterized by it, can set off in the learner an ever-increasing creative curiosity. What I'm really saying is this: The more critically one exercises one's capacity for learning, the greater is one's capacity for constructing and developing what I call "epistemological curiosity,"[2] without which it is not possible to obtain a complete grasp of the object of our knowledge.

This understanding of epistemological curiosity brings us, on the one hand, to a critique and a refusal of the "banking system" of education,[3] and, on the other hand, to an understanding that, even when submitted to this system that is a deformation of the creativity of both learners and teachers, the learners are not necessarily fated to stagnate. Not because of the "teaching" they have received but because of the very process of learning itself, learners can circumvent and outmaneuver the authoritarianism and the epistemological error of this "banking system."

What is essential is that learners, though subjected to the praxis of the "banking system," maintain alive the flame of resistance that sharpens their curiosity and stimulates their capacity for risk, for adventure, so as to immunize themselves against the banking system. In this sense, the creative force of the learning process, which encompasses comparison, repetition, observation, indomitable doubt, and curiosity not easily satisfied, overcomes the negative effects of false teaching. This capacity to go beyond the factors of conditioning is one of the obvious advantages of the human person. Of course, this capacity does not mean that it is a matter of indifference to us whether we become a "banking system" educator or one whose role is essentially to "problematize," to use the critical faculty.

Methodological Rigor

The educator with a democratic vision or posture cannot avoid in his teaching praxis insisting on the critical capacity, curiosity, and autonomy of the learner. One of the essential tasks of the teaching process is to introduce the learners to the methodological exactitude with which they should approach the learning process, through which the objects of learning are knowable. And this methodological exactitude has nothing to do with the discourse of the "banking system," something that merely touches the surface of the object or its contents. It's exactly in this sense that to teach cannot be reduced to a superficial or externalized contact with the object or its content but extends to the production of the conditions in which critical learning is possible. These conditions imply and demand the presence of teaching and learning simultaneously in the context of a rigorous methodological curiosity anxious to explore the limits of creativity, persistent in the search, and courageously humble in the adventure. In these conditions, those who are engaged in critical learning know that their teachers are continuously in the process of acquiring new knowledge and that this new knowledge cannot simply be transferred to them, the learners. At the same time, in the context of true learning, the learners will be engaged in a continuous transformation through which they become authentic subjects of the construction and reconstruction of what is being taught, side by side with the teacher, who is equally subject to the same process. Only in this way can we speak authentically of knowledge that is taught, in which the taught is grasped in its very essence and, therefore, learned by those who are learning.

Thus it becomes clear that the role of the educator is one of a tranquil possession of certitude in regard to the teaching not only of contents but also of "correct thinking." Therefore, it becomes obvious that she/he will never develop a truly "critical" perspective as a teacher by indulging in mechanical memorization or the rhythmic repetition of phrases and ideas at the expense of creative challenge. Intellectuals who memorize everything, reading for hours on end, slaves to the text, fearful of taking a risk, speaking as if they were reciting from memory, fail to make any concrete connections between what they have read and what is happening in the world, the country, or the local community. They repeat what has been read with precision but rarely teach anything of personal value. They speak correctly about dialectical thought but think mechanistically. Such teachers inhabit an idealized world, a world of mere data, disconnected from the one most people inhabit.

It's not possible to read critically if one treats reading as if it were a similar operation to buying in bulk. What's the point of boasting of having read twenty books—twenty books! Really reading involves a kind of relationship with the text, which offers itself to me and to which I give myself and through the fundamental comprehension of which I undergo the process of becoming a subject. While reading, I'm not just a captive of the mind of the text as if it were simply a product of its author. This is a vitiated form of reading that has nothing to do with thinking or teaching correctly.

In fact, the person who thinks "correctly," even if at times she/he thinks wrongly, is the only one capable of teaching "correct" thinking. For one of the necessary requirements for correct thinking is a capacity for not being overly convinced of one's own certitudes. Taking into account the need for a rigorous ethical purity totally distinct from Puritanism (in other words, an ethical purity that generates beauty), correct thinking is in this sense irreconcilable with self-conceited arrogance.

The teacher who thinks "correctly" transmits to the students the beauty of our way of existing in the world as historical beings, capable of intervening in and knowing this world. Historical as we are, our knowledge of the world has historicity. It transmits, in addition, that our knowing and our knowledge are the fruit of historicity. And that knowledge, when newly produced, replaces what before was new but is now old and ready to be surpassed by the coming of a new dawn.[4] Therefore, it is as necessary to be immersed in existing knowledge as it is to be open and capable of producing something that does not yet exist. And these two moments of the epistemological process are accounted for in teaching, learning, and doing research. The one moment, in which knowledge that already exists is taught and learned, and the other, in which the production of what is not yet known is the object of research. Thus, the teaching-learning process, together with the work of research, is essential and an inseparable aspect of the gnostic cycle.

Research

Once again, there is no such thing as teaching without research and research without teaching.[5] One inhabits the body of the other. As I teach, I continue to search and re-search. I teach because I search, because I question, and because I submit myself to questioning. I research because I notice things, take cognizance of them. And in so doing, I intervene. And intervening, I educate and educate myself. I do research so as to know what I do not yet know and to communicate and proclaim what I discover.

To think correctly, in critical terms, is a requirement imposed by the rhythms of the gnostic circle on our curiosity, which, as it becomes more methodologically rigorous, progresses from ingenuity to what I have called "epistemological curiosity." Ingenuous curiosity, from which there results, without doubt, a certain kind of knowledge (even though not methodologically rigorous) is what characterizes "common sense" knowing. It is knowledge extracted from pure experience. To think correctly, from the teacher's point of view, implies respect for "common sense" knowing as it progresses from "common sense" to its higher stage. It also implies respect and stimulus for the creative capacity of the learner. It further implies a commitment on the part of educators and teachers that respects the critical consciousness of the learner, in the knowledge that the ingenuous consciousness of the learner will not be overcome automatically.

Respect for What Students Know

For this reason, thinking correctly puts the responsibility on the teacher, or, more correctly, on the school, not only to respect the kinds of knowledge that exist especially among the popular classes—knowledge socially constructed in communitarian praxis—but also (as I've been saying for thirty years) to discuss with the students the logic of these kinds of knowledge in relation to their contents.

Why not, for example, take advantage of the students' experience of life in those parts of the city neglected by the authorities to discuss the problems of pollution in the rivers and the question of poverty and the risks to health from the rubbish heaps in such areas? Why are there no rubbish heaps in the heart of the rich areas of the city? This question is considered "in bad taste." Pure demagogy. Almost subversive, say the defenders of democracy.

Why not discuss with the students the concrete reality of their lives and that aggressive reality in which violence is permanent and where people are much more familiar with death than with life? Why not establish an "intimate" connection between knowledge considered basic to any school curriculum and knowledge that is the fruit of the lived experience of these students as individuals? Why not discuss the implications, political and ideological, of the neglect of the poor areas of the city by the constituted authorities? Are there class-related ethical questions that need to be looked at here? A pragmatic reactionary educator would probably say that there is no connection between one thing and the other. That the school is not the Party. That the function of the school is to teach and transfer contents—packages—to the students, which, once learned, will operate automatically.

A Capacity to Be Critical

It is my conviction that the difference and the distance between ingenuity and critical thinking, between knowledge resulting from pure experience and that resulting from rigorous methodological procedure, do not constitute a rupture but a sort of further stage in the knowing process. This further stage, which is a continuity rather than a rupture, happens when ingenuous curiosity, while remaining curious, becomes capable of self-criticism. In criticizing itself, ingenuous curiosity becomes "epistemological curiosity," as through greater methodological exactitude it appropriates the object of its knowing.

In truth, ingenuous, "unarmed" curiosity, which is associated with common sense knowledge, is the same curiosity that, as it develops its critical possibilities through a more rigorous methodological approximation of the known object, becomes epistemological curiosity. It changes in quality but not in essence. The curiosity of simple rural people with whom I have been in dialogue throughout my politico-pedagogical career, whether fatalist or rebellious in the face of the violence of injustice, is the same curiosity, in the sense of a kind of awe or wonder in the presence of the "not I," common to scientists or philosophers as they contemplate the world. Scientists and philosophers, however, overcome the ingenuous curiosity of simple folk and become "epistemologically" curious.

Curiosity as restless questioning, as movement toward the revelation of something hidden, as a question verbalized or not, as search for clarity, as a moment of attention, suggestion, and vigilance, constitutes an integral part of the phenomenon of being alive. There could be no creativity without the curiosity that moves us and sets us patiently impatient before a world that we did not make, to add to it something of our own making.

In fact, human curiosity, as a phenomenon present to all vital experience, is in a permanent process of social and historical construction and reconstruction. It's precisely because ingenuous curiosity does not automatically become critical that one of the essential tasks of progressive educational praxis is the promotion of a curiosity that is critical, bold, and adventurous. A type of curiosity that can defend us from the excess of a rationality that now inundates our highly technologized world. Which does not mean that we are to adopt a false humanist posture of denying the value of technology and science. On the contrary, it's a posture of balance that neither deifies nor demonizes technology. A posture that is from those who consider technology from a critically curious standpoint.

Ethics and Aesthetics

Further, the necessary process from ingenuous to critical curiosity should also be accompanied by a rigorous ethical formation side by side with an aesthetic appreciation. Beauty and decency, hand in hand. I am more and more convinced that educational praxis, while avoiding the trap of puritanical moralism, cannot avoid the task of becoming a clear witness to decency and purity. That is, it cannot avoid the task of being a permanent critique of the easy solutions that tempt us away from the true path that we need to construct and follow. As men and women inserted in and formed by a socio-historical context of relations, we become capable of comparing, evaluating, intervening, deciding, taking new directions, and thereby constituting ourselves as ethical beings. It is in our becoming that we constitute our being so. Because the condition of becoming is the condition of being. In addition, it is not possible to imagine the human condition disconnected from the ethical condition. Because to be disconnected from it or to regard it as irrelevant constitutes for us women and men a transgression. For this reason, to transform the experience of educating into a matter of simple technique is to impoverish what is fundamentally human in this experience: namely, its capacity to form the human person. If we have any serious regard for what it means to be human, the teaching of contents cannot be separated from the moral formation of the learners. To educate is essentially to form. To deify or demonize technology[6] or science is an extremely negative way of thinking incorrectly. To act in front of students as if the truth belongs only to the teacher is not only preposterous but also false. To think correctly demands profundity and not superficiality in the comprehension and interpretation of the facts. It presupposes an openness that allows for the revision of conclusions; it recognizes not only the possibility of making a new choice or a new evaluation but also the *right* to do so. However, since there can be no "right thinking" disconnected from ethical principles, it is also clear that the demands of "right thinking" require that the possibility or the right to change be not simply rhetorical. In other words, to claim the right to change requires a coherence that makes a difference. There is no point in making such a claim and continuing as if nothing had changed.

Words Incarnated in Example

The teacher who really teaches, that is, who really works with contents within the context of methodological exactitude, will deny as false the hypocritical formula, "do as I say, not as I do." Whoever is engaged in "right thinking" knows only too well that words not given body (made flesh) have little or no value. Right thinking is right doing.

What are serious students to think of a teacher who for two semesters spoke passionately about the necessity for popular movements to struggle for their autonomy and who today, denying that he has changed, indulges in pragmatic attacks against these same popular classes, attributing little or no value to their utopias, and who himself fully engaged in transferring his own knowledge to his students à la banking system. What can be said of the teacher who until recently, as a member of a leftist party, defended the necessity of education for the working classes and who now, resigned fatalistically to neoliberal pragmatism, is satisfied with the simple professional training of the unemployed, while considering that he is still "progressive" pedagogically and politically?

There is no right thinking that can be separated from a kind of coherent, lived practice that is capable of reformulating contents and paradigms instead of simply negating what is no longer regarded as relevant. It is absurd for teachers to imagine that they are engaged in right thinking and at the same time to relate to the student in a patronizing way.

The attitude, which is a way of being and not just an occasional phase, of the teacher engaged in right thinking demands a seriousness in the search for secure and solid bases for his/her positions. A teacher with such an attitude, while capable of disagreeing with an opponent, does not harbor rancor against that person in such a way that the rancor assumes proportions greater than the reasons for the original disagreement. Once, one such rancorous person forbade a student who was doing a dissertation on literacy and citizenship from reading any of my works. "He is old hat," was the rigorously "neutral" way that he dismissed the "object" that was myself. "If you read his work you will end up the worse for it," was his concluding remark to the student. That is no way to be engaged in right thinking or in right teaching.[7] Integral to right thinking is a generous heart, one that, while not denying the right to anger, can distinguish it from cynicism or unbalanced fury.

Risk, Acceptance of What Is New, and Rejection of Discrimination

Proper to right thinking is a willingness to risk, to welcome the new, which cannot be rejected simply because it is new no more than the old can be rejected because chronologically it is no longer new. The old is capable of remaining new when it remains faithful through time to the experience of original and founding intuitions and inspirations.

It is equally part of right thinking to reject decidedly any and every form of discrimination. Preconceptions of race, class, or sex offend the essence of human dignity and constitute a radical negation of democracy. How far from these values we are when we tolerate the impunity of those who kill a street child; those who murder peasants who struggle for a minimum of justice; those who discriminate on the basis of color, burning churches where blacks pray because prayer is only white; those who treat women as inferior beings; and so on. I feel more pity than rage at the absurd arrogance of this kind of white supremacy, passing itself off to the world as democracy. In fact, this form of thinking and doing is far removed from the humility demanded by "right" thinking. Nor has it anything to do with the good sense that keeps our exaggerations in check and helps us avoid falling into the ridiculous and the senseless.

There are times when I fear that someone reading this, even if not yet totally converted to neoliberal pragmatism but perhaps somewhat contaminated by it, may think that there is no more place among us for the dreamer and the believer in utopia. Yet what I have been saying up to now is not the stuff of inconsequential dreamers. It has to do with the very nature of men and women as makers and dreamers of history and not simply as casualties of an a priori vision of the world.[8]

Given my understanding of human nature, I have no option but to defend the position I have been defending all along. It's a demand about right thinking that I make on myself as I write this text. The demand, that is, that right thinking belongs intimately to right doing. In this sense, to teach right thinking is not something that is simply spoken of or an experience that is merely described. But something that is done and lived while it is being spoken of, as if the doing and living of it constituted a kind of irrefutable witness of its truth. To think correctly implies the existence of subjects whose thinking is mediated by objects that provoke and modify the thinking subject. Thinking correctly is, in other words, not an isolated act or something to draw near in isolation but an act of communication. For this reason, there is no right thinking without understanding, and this understanding, from a correct thinking point of view, is not something transferred but something that belongs essentially to the process of coparticipation. If, from the grammatical point of view, the verb to understand is "transitive," in relation to a correct way of thinking it is also a verb whose subject is always a coparticipant with the other. All understanding, if it is not mechanistically treated, that is, submitted to the alienating care that threatens the mind and that I have been designating as a "bureaucratized" mind, necessarily implies communicability. There is no knowing (that is, connecting one thing to another) something that is not at the same time a "communication" of the something known (unless, of course, the process of knowing has broken down). The act of a correct way of thinking does not "transfer," "deposit," "offer," or "donate" to the other as if the receiver were a passive object of facts, concepts, and intelligibility. To be coherent, the educator who thinks correctly, exercising as a human subject the incontestable practice of comprehension, challenges the learner with whom and to whom she/he communicates to produce her or his understanding of what is being communicated. There is no intelligibility that is not at the same time communication and intercommunication, and that is not grounded in dialogue.

For this reason, a correct way of thinking is dialogical and not polemical.

Critical Reflection on Practice

A correct way of thinking knows, for example, that the practice of critical teaching is not built as if thinking correctly were a mere given. However, it knows that without a correct way of thinking, there can be no critical practice. In other words, the practice of critical teaching, implicit in a correct way of thinking, involves a dynamic and dialectical movement between "doing" and "reflecting on doing." The knowledge produced by spontaneous or almost spontaneous teaching practice is ingenuous in the sense that it lacks the methodological rigor that characterizes the epistemological curiosity of a reflecting subject. Such knowledge is not what disciplined, correct thinking seeks. For this reason it is essential that during the experience of teaching preparation, the prospective teacher must realize that a correct way of thinking is not a gift from heaven, nor is it to be found in teachers' guide books, put there by illuminated intellectuals who occupy the center of power. On the contrary, a correct way of thinking that goes beyond the ingenuous must be produced by the learners in communion with the teacher responsible for their education. At the same time, it is necessary to insist that the matrix both of ingenuous and critical thinking is the same curiosity that characterizes all human vitality. In this sense, the untrained teachers in rural areas around Pernambuco, Brazil, or in any of the world's "remote" places, are as curious as the professor of philosophy of education in any university. All that is necessary is that, through reflection on a given practice, ingenuous curiosity perceive itself as such so as to advance to the critical stage.

For this reason, in the process of the ongoing education of teachers, the essential moment is that of critical reflection on one's practice.

Thinking critically about practice, of today or yesterday, makes possible the improvement of tomorrow's practice. Even theoretical discourse itself, necessary as it is to critical reflection, must be concrete enough to be clearly identifiable with practice. Its epistemological "distance" from practice as an object of analysis ought to be compensated for by an even greater proximity to the object of analysis, in terms of lived experience. The better this process is accomplished, the greater is the gain in intelligence and the greater the possibility of communicability in overcoming an ingenuous attitude toward knowledge. In addition, the more I acknowledge my own process and attitudes and perceive the reasons behind these, the more I am capable of changing and advancing from the stage of ingenuous curiosity to epistemological curiosity. It's really not possible for someone to imagine himself/herself as a subject in the process of becoming without having at the same time a disposition for change. And change of which she/he is not merely the victim but the subject.

It is an idealistic exaggeration, for example, to imagine that the objective threat that smoking poses to anyone's health and to my life is enough to make me stop smoking. Of course, the objective threat is contextually essential if I am to take any steps at all. But such a threat will only become a "subjective" decision to the degree that it generates new options that can provoke a break with past habits and an acceptance of new commitments: When I assume consciously the danger represented by smoking, I am then moved to reflect on its consequences and to engage in a decision-making process, leading to a break, an option, which becomes concretized, materially speaking, in the practice of "not smoking," a practice grounded on the risk to health and life implicit in smoking.

There is another fundamental element here too: the emotional one. In other words, in addition to the knowledge I have of the harm smoking does to me, I now have, through the consciousness I have acquired of this harm, a sense of legitimate anger. In addition, I have a sense of joy that I was able to be angry because it means that I can continue to live a while longer in the world. The kind of education that does not recognize the right to express appropriate anger against injustice, against disloyalty, against the negation of love, against exploitation, and against violence fails to see the educational role implicit in the expression of these feelings. One thinks of Christ's anger against the merchants in the temple. Of those who struggle for agrarian reform against the enemies of agrarian reform. Of the victims of violence and of discrimination based on class, race, and sex. Of those whose victimization cannot be vindicated because of the perpetrator's impunity. Of those who go hungry against those who not only eat well but also waste food, as if life belonged to them alone. However, it's important to stress the "appropriateness" of this anger; otherwise it simply degenerates into rage and even hatred.

Cultural Identity

It's interesting to take a close look at the verb "to assume," which is a transitive verb and can have as its object the person who assumes his or herself. For example, I can assume the risk inherent in smoking just as much as I can assume myself (what I am) as the subject and object of that assumption. When I say that in order to stop smoking it is essential that I assume that smoking constitutes a risk to my life, what I am really saying is that I have acquired a complete and clear picture of what smoking is and what its consequences are. A more radical sense of "to assume" is when I say: One of the most important tasks of critical educational practice is to make possible the conditions in which the learners, in their interaction with one another and with their teachers, engage in the experience of assuming themselves as social, historical, thinking, communicating, transformative, creative persons; dreamers of possible utopias, capable of being angry because of a capacity to love. Capable of assuming themselves as "subject" because of the capacity to recognize themselves as "object." All this, while bearing in mind that the assumption of oneself does not signify the exclusion of others. Because it is the otherness of the "not I" or the "you" that makes me assume the radicality of the "I." There's another question that cannot be overlooked either, namely, the question of cultural identity in relation to both individuals and classes among the learners and for which (in the context of forward-looking educational practice) respect is absolutely fundamental. It is connected directly to the challenge of assuming who we are, which is what a purely technical, objective, and grammatical vision of education cannot do or be.

The historical, political, social, and cultural experience of men and women can never be acquired outside of the conflict between those forces that are dedicated to the prevention of self-assumption on the part of individuals and groups and those forces that work in favor of such an assumption. Teaching preparation that considers itself to be above such "intrigues" does nothing less than work in favor of the obstacles to self-assumption. The socio-political solidarity that we need today to build a less ugly and less intolerant human community where we can be really what we are cannot neglect the importance of democratic practice. Purely pragmatic training, with its implicit or openly expressed elitist authoritarianism, is incompatible with the learning and practice of becoming a "subject."

Sometimes a simple, almost insignificant gesture on the part of a teacher can have a profound formative effect on the life of a student. I will always remember one such gesture in my life when I was an adolescent. A gesture that marks me profoundly but whose significance on my life was almost certainly not noticed or known by my teacher. At that time I experienced myself as an insecure adolescent, not at home with a body perceived as more bone than beauty, feeling myself to be less capable than the other students, insecure about my own creative possibilities, easily riled, and not very much at peace with the world. The slightest gesture by any of the better-off students in the class was capable of highlighting my insecurity and my fragility.

On this occasion our teacher had brought our homework to school after correcting it and was calling us one by one to comment on it. When my turn came, I noticed he was looking over my text with great attention, nodding his head in an attitude of respect and consideration. His respectful and appreciative attitude had a much greater effect on me than the high classification that he gave me for my work. The gesture of the teacher affirmed in me a self-confidence that obviously still had much room to grow. But it inspired in me a belief that I too had value and could work and produce results— results that clearly had their limits but that were a demonstration of my capacity, which up until that moment I would have been inclined to hide or not fully believe in. And the greatest proof of the importance of that gesture is that I can speak of it now as if it had happened only today.

The importance of the kind of knowledge transmitted by gestures such as these, which are part and parcel of daily school life, needs serious reflection. It's a pity that the socializing character of the school, with its multiple possibilities for formation or deformation, especially in the context of the ordinary informality of the day to day, is so much neglected. What we mostly hear about is the teaching of contents, understood almost always, unfortunately, as the transference of knowledge. One of the reasons, in my view, for this negligence is a too narrow understanding of what education and learning are. Really, it has not yet dawned on us that education is something that women and men discovered experimentally, in the course of history. If it were clear to us that our capacity to teach arose from our capacity to learn, we would easily have understood the importance of informal experiences in the street, in the square, in the work place, in the classroom, in the playground, among the school staff of both teachers and administrative personnel. There is strong "witness" potential in all of these informal situations, but it is, practically speaking, unexplored territory. In "Education in the City,"[9] I drew attention to this fact when I discovered the calamitous state of the education system that Luíza Erundina encountered when she took up office in 1989 as mayor of São Paulo, Brazil. On my first visits to the city schools, I saw the calamity with my own eyes and I was terrified. The whole system was a disaster, from the state of the buildings and the classrooms to the quality of the teaching. How was it possible to ask of the children the minimum of respect for their material surroundings when the authorities demonstrated such absolute neglect of and indifference to the public institutions under their care? It's really unbelievable that we are unable to include all these elements in our "rhetoric" about education. Why does such "rhetoric" not include hygiene, cleanliness, beauty? Why does it neglect the indisputable pedagogical value of the "materiality" of the school environment?

Yet, it is such detail in the daily life both of teacher and student, to which so little attention is given, that in fact possesses significant weight in the evaluation of teaching practice. What is important in teaching is not the mechanical repetition of this or that gesture but a comprehension of the value of sentiments, emotions, and desires. Of the insecurity that can only be overcome by inspiring confidence. Of the fear that can only be abated to the degree that courage takes its place.

There is no true teaching preparation possible separated from a critical attitude that spurs ingenuous curiosity to become epistemological curiosity, together with a recognition of the value of emotions, sensibility, affectivity, and intuition. To know is not simply to intuit or to have a hunch, though there is an intimate connection between them. We must build on our intuitions and submit them to methodical and rigorous analysis so that our curiosity becomes epistemological.[10]

THREE

TEACHING IS NOT JUST
TRANSFERRING KNOWLEDGE

The considerations and reflections I have been making up to now are developments of an initial insight that is fundamental to progressive teaching principles. Namely, that to know how to teach is to create possibilities for the construction and production of knowledge rather than to be engaged simply in a game of transferring knowledge. When I enter a classroom I should be someone who is open to new ideas, open to questions, and open to the curiosities of the students as well as their inhibitions. In other words, I ought to be aware of being a critical and inquiring subject in regard to the task entrusted to me, the task of teaching and not that of transferring knowledge.

It is important to insist on this point, to insist on this kind of teaching as necessary to being a teacher and as necessary to everyone in education. And to understand its ontological, political, ethical, epistemological, and pedagogical basis. It is also important that it be something witnessed, lived.

As a teacher in an education program, I cannot be satisfied simply with nice, theoretical elaborations regarding the ontological, political, and epistemological bases of educational practice. My theoretical explanation of such practice ought to be also a concrete and practical demonstration of what I am saying. A kind of incarnation joining theory and practice. In speaking of the construction of knowledge, I ought to be involved practically, incarnationally, in such construction and be involving the student in it also.

Otherwise I fall into a net of contradictions that loses any power to convince. I become as inauthentic as someone who talks about creating a climate of equality in the school while behaving like an autocrat. Or, as inauthentic as someone who talks about combating racism but who, when asked if she/he knows Madalena, a black female student, replies: "Yes, I know her. She is black, but she's a decent soul." I've never heard anyone say: "I know Célia, she is blond with blue eyes, but she's decent all the same." In the phrase regarding Madalena, the black person, we find the adversative conjunction "but." In the phrase about fair-haired and blue-eyed Célia, the adversative conjunction sounds redundant. The use of conjunctions in a sentence establishes a relationship of causality, for example: "I speak *because* I refuse to be silent." Or a relationship of adversity, for example: "They tried to dominate him *but* they could not." Or a relationship of finality, for example: "Peter struggled *so that* he might make his position clear." Or a relationship of integration, for example: "Pedro knew *that* he would return." So, really, there are many different uses of the adversative conjunction, and it is clear that the use of the adversative *but* in relation to Madalena is ideologically based because of her color. In other words, a black person in general could hardly be expected to be decent or competent. Whenever a black person is found to be decent and competent our innate racism draws on the adversative conjunction *but* to acknowledge what is clearly an exception to the rule. In the case of Célia, blue eyed and fair haired, there is no innate suspicion of her being lacking in decency or competence, hence the use of the adversarial conjunction *but* is tautological. The wide question here, then, is ideological, not grammatical.

To think correctly and to know that to teach is not merely to transfer knowledge is a demanding and difficult discipline, at times a burden that we have to carry with others, for others, and for ourselves. It is difficult, not because right thinking is the property of angels and saints and something to which we aspire only if we are arrogant. It is difficult because it demands constant vigilance over ourselves so as to avoid being simplistic, facile, and incoherent. It is difficult because we are not always sufficiently balanced to prevent legitimate anger from degenerating into the kind of rage that breeds false and erroneous thinking. No matter how much someone may irritate me, I have no right to puff myself up with my own self-importance so as to declare that person to be absolutely incompetent, assuming a posture of disdain from my own position of false superiority. I, for example, do not feel anger but pity when angry people, full of their own genius, minimize me and make little of me.

For example, it's tiring to live the kind of humility that is the sine qua non of right thinking and the very basis from which we can admit our own mistakes and allow ourselves to diminish so that others may increase.

The climate of right thinking has nothing to do with preestablished formulae, yet it would be a negation of right thinking to imagine that it could flourish in an atmosphere of indiscipline or mere "spontaneity." Without methodological rigor, there can be no right thinking.

Awareness of Our Unfinishedness

As a teacher with critical acumen, I do not cease to be a responsible "adventurer" disposed to accept change and difference. Nothing of what I experienced as a teacher needs to be repeated. However, I hold that my own unity and identity, in regard to others and to the world, constitutes my essential and irrepeatable way of experiencing myself as a cultural, historical, and unfinished being in the world, simultaneously conscious of my unfinishedness.

And here we have arrived at the point from which perhaps we should have departed: the unfinishedness of our being. In fact, this unfinishedness is essential to our human condition. Whenever there is life, there is unfinishedness, though only among women and men is it possible to speak of an awareness of unfinishedness. The invention of our existence developed through our interaction with the material world at our disposal, creating a life support in which life, the life of women and men, became sustainable. Within this life support, our life, human life, takes on a specific qualitative difference in relation to animal life. Animals, for example, operate in given dimensions of space, confined in some cases, unrestricted in others, in which they develop "affective" boundaries necessary for their survival, growth, and development. It's the space where they, trained and skilled, "learn" the skills of hunting, attacking, and self-defense, in a period of time much shorter than human learners do. The greater the gap, culturally speaking, the greater the time of learning of "infancy." The nonhuman animals in the infrastructural support system do not have a conceptual language, that is, the capacity to "grasp" consciously the implication that belonging to an infrastructure would inevitably endow them with the capacity to communicate a certain awe in the face of life itself, in the face of its mystery. In this sense, their behavior, within the context of the spacio-temporal infrastructure, is explicable in reference to the species to which individual animals belong rather than in reference to the individual itself. That is, the individual does not have the freedom to opt. For this reason, we cannot speak of ethical questions in regard to elephants, for example.

This basic life infrastructure or life support system did not require or imply the use of language or the erect posture that would free the hands—the two things that in fact would make possible the emergence of *Homo sapiens*. The more the hands and the brain engaged in a sort of pact of solidarity, the more the support system become "world," "life," "existence." In other words, as the human body became aware of the capacity of "capture," "learn," "transform," and to create beauty, it ceased to be simply empty "space" to be filled in with contents.

The invention of "existence" necessarily involves the emergence of language, culture, and communication at levels of complexity much greater than that which obtains at the level of survival, self-defense, and self-preservation. What makes men and women ethical is their capacity to "spiritualize" the world, to make it either beautiful or ugly. Their capacity to intervene, to compare, to judge, to decide, to choose, to desist makes them capable of acts of greatness, of dignity, and, at the same time, of the unthinkable in terms of indignity. It's not possible to break with an ethical code unless one has become an ethical being. It is unknown for lions to cowardly murder lions of the same family group, or of another group, and afterwards to visit the families to offer them their condolences. It is unknown for African tigers to throw highly destructive bombs on "cities" of Asiatic tigers.

While *Homo sapiens* were emerging from the basic life-support structure, intervening creatively in the world, they invented language to be able to give a name to things that resulted from its intervention, "grasping" intellectuality and being able to communicate what had been "grasped." It was becoming simultaneously clear that human existence is, in fact, a radical and profound tension between good and evil, between dignity and indignity, between decency and indecency, between the beauty and the ugliness of the world. In other words, it was becoming clear that it is impossible to humanly exist without assuming the right and the duty to opt, to decide, to struggle, to be political. All of which brings us back again to the preeminence of education experience and to its eminently ethical character, which in its turn leads us to the radical nature of "hope." In other words, though I know that things can get worse, I also know that I am able to intervene to improve them.

I like being human, being a person, precisely because it is not already given as certain, unequivocal, or irrevocable that I am or will be "correct," that I will bear witness to what is authentic, that I am or will be just, that I will respect others, that I will not lie and thereby diminish the value of others because of my envy or even anger of their questioning my presence in the world. I like being human because I know that my passing through the world is not predetermined, preestablished. That my destiny is not a given but something that needs to be constructed and for which I must assume responsibility. I like being human because I am involved with others in making history out of possibility, not simply resigned to fatalistic stagnation. Consequently, the future is something to be constructed through trial and error rather than an inexorable vice that determines all our actions.

Recognition of One's Conditioning

I like to be human because in my unfinishedness I know that I am conditioned. Yet conscious of such conditioning, I know that I can go beyond it, which is the essential difference between conditioned and determined existence. The difference between the unfinished that does not know anything of such a condition, and the unfinished who socio-historically has arrived at the point of becoming conscious of the condition and unfinishedness. I like being human because I perceive that the construction of my presence in the world, which is a construction involving others and is subject to genetic factors that I have inherited and to socio-cultural and historical factors, is nonetheless a presence whose construction has much to do with myself. It would be ironic if the awareness of my presence in the world did not at the same time imply a recognition that I could not be absent from the construction of my own presence. I cannot perceive myself as a presence in the world and at the same time explain it as the result of forces completely alien to me. If I do so, I simply renounce my historical, ethical, social, and political responsibility for my own evolution from the life-support system to the emergence of *Homo sapiens*. In that sense, I renounce my ontological vocation to intervene in the world. The fact that I perceive myself to be in the world, with the world, with others, brings with it a sense of "being-with" constitutive of who I am that makes my relationship to the world essential to who I am. In other words, my presence in the world is not so much of someone who is merely adapting to something "external," but of someone who is inserted as if belonging essentially to it. It's the position of one who struggles to become the subject and maker of history and not simply a passive, disconnected object.

I like being a human person because even though I know that the material, social, political, cultural, and ideological conditions in which we find ourselves almost always generate divisions that make difficult the construction of our ideals of change and transformation, I know also that the obstacles are not eternal.

In the 1960s, when I reflected on these obstacles I called for "conscientization," not as a panacea but as an attempt at critical awareness of those obstacles and their raison d'être. And, in the face of pragmatic, reactionary, and fatalistic neoliberal philosophizing, I still insist, without falling into the trap of "idealism," on the absolute necessity of conscientization. In truth, conscientization is a requirement of our human condition. It is one of the roads we have to follow if we are to deepen our awareness of our world, of facts, of events, of the demands of human consciousness to develop our capacity for epistemological curiosity. Far from being alien to our human condition, conscientization is natural to "unfinished" humanity that is aware of its unfinishedness. It is natural because unfinishedness is integral to the phenomenon of life itself, which besides women and men includes the cherry trees in my garden and the birds that sing in their branches. Or my German shepherd Eico who happily "greets" me every morning.

Among us women and men, we recognize our unfinishedness. And this awareness necessarily implies our insertion in a permanent process of search, motivated by a curiosity that surpasses the limits that are peculiar to the life phenomenon as such, becoming progressively the ground and foundation for the production of knowledge, for that curiosity is already knowledge.

Not so long ago, my wife Nita and I were waiting for a plane in an airport in Brazil's northeast. It was a red-eye flight down to São Paulo. We were very tired and regretted not having changed our flight plans. Eventually we settled down and became calm, mainly due to the presence of a small child who ran about happily, motivated by curiosity and wonder. Pricking his ears at the sound of the plane's engines approaching, he announces to his delighted mother that the plane is arriving. She confirms his discovery. So, off with him to the end of the departure lounge to exercise his curiosity at even closer range. Returning, he announces with even greater certainty and delight, "The plane has already landed."

So here we have an interesting demonstration of curiosity leading to knowledge. First, the child, impelled by his curiosity, processes the sounds of the engines in the context of "waiting" and deduces the knowledge or fact that the plane is approaching. Second, using the adverb "already," he temporalizes the arrival and is able to deduce that it has in fact landed or arrived. So, these two moments in the process of the child's knowing are products of the concreteness of the facts and the command he is able to exercise in relation to the notion of time, expressed by the adverb "already."

Returning for a moment to what we were saying before, we recall that our awareness of our unfinishedness makes us responsible beings, hence the notion of our presence in the world as ethical. We recall also that it is only because we are ethical that we can also be unethical. The world of culture, which is also the world of history, is the world where freedom, choice, decision, and possibility are only possible because they can also be denied, despised, or refused. For this reason, the education of women and men can never be purely instrumental. It must also necessarily be ethical. The obviousness of this requirement is such that it should not even be necessary to insist on it in the context of technical and scientific education. However, it's essential to insist on it because, as unfinished beings, conscious of our unfinishedness, we are capable of options and decisions that may not be ethical. The teacher of geography who truncates the curiosity of the student in the name of the efficiency of mechanical memorization hampers both the freedom and the capacity for adventure of the student. There is no education here. Only domestication.

Such domestication is little different from the fatalistic ideology current in neoliberal thought, the victims of which are, of course, the popular classes. The excuse is that nothing can be done to alter the course of events. Unemployment, for example, is inevitable as the world moves into a new end-of-the-century era. Yet the same fatalism does not apply when it is a question of trillions of dollars chasing each other around the globe with the rapidity of faxes, in an insatiable search for even greater profits. In the context of agrarian reform, here in Brazil those who "own" the world talk about the need to discipline, to "soften," at any cost, the rowdy and turbulent movement of the landless people. And, of course, land reform itself is far from being inevitable. Only disloyal Brazilians and troublemakers propose such an absurd idea.

Let's continue a little longer to reflect on the question of incompleteness. And of the incompleteness that knows itself to be so, which is our case but not the case of the animals. This incompleteness implies for us a permanent movement of search. In fact, it would be a contradiction if we who are aware of our incompleteness were not involved in a movement of constant search. For this reason, women and men by the mere fact of being *in* the world are also necessarily being *with* world. Our being is a *being with*. So, to be in the world without making history, without being made by it, without creating culture, without a sensibility toward one's own presence in the world, without a dream, without song, music, or painting, without caring for the earth or the water, without using one's hands, without sculpting or philosophizing, without any opinion about the world, without doing science or theology, without awe in the face of mystery, without learning, instruction, teaching, without ideas on education, without being political, is a total impossibility.

It is in our incompleteness, of which we are aware, that education as a permanent process is grounded. Women and men are capable of being educated only to the extent that they are capable of recognizing themselves as unfinished. Education does not make us educable. It is our awareness of being unfinished that makes us educable. And the same awareness in which we are inserted makes us eternal seekers. Eternal because of hope. Hope is not just a question of grit or courage. It's an ontological dimension of our human condition.[1]

This is a fundamental foundation of our educational practice, of our teaching preparation. Ideally, educators, students, and prospective teachers should together be conversant with other forms of knowledge that are seldom part of the curriculum. They should incorporate into their way of life the ideal of permanent hope-giving search, which is one of the fruits of our essential (and assumed) unfinishedness. A fruit that begins as knowledge and that with time is transformed into wisdom. Something that should be in no way strange to us as educators. When I leave the house to go to work with students, there is no doubt at all in my mind that, given an openness to curiosity, to search, to hearing, based on awareness of our unfin-ishedness, "programmed but to learn,"[2] we will exercise our capacity to learn and to teach so much the better for being subjects and not simply objects of the process we are engaged in.

Respect for the Autonomy of the Student

Another kind of knowledge necessary to educational practice and grounded in the same principles as those just discussed is the knowledge that speaks of respect for the autonomy of the learner, whether the learner be child, youth, or adult. As an educator, I have to constantly remind myself of this knowledge because it is connected with the affirmation of respect for myself. This principle, once again, is a question of the ethical implications of being an unfinished being. Respect for the autonomy and dignity of every person is an ethical imperative and not a favor that we may or may not concede to each other. It is precisely because we are ethical beings that we can commit what can only be called a transgression by denying our essentially ethical condition. The teacher who does not respect the student's curiosity in its diverse aesthetic, linguistic, and syntactical expressions; who uses irony to put down legitimate questioning (recognizing of course that freedom is not absolute, that it requires of its nature certain limits); who is not respectfully present in the educational experience of the student, transgresses fundamental ethical principles of the human condition. It is in this sense that both the authoritarian teacher who suffocates the natural curiosity and freedom of the student as well as the teacher who imposes no standards at all are equally disrespectful of an essential characteristic of our humanness, namely, our radical (and assumed) unfinishedness, out of which emerges the possibility of being ethical. It is also in this sense that the possibility of true dialogue, in which subjects in dialogue learn and grow by confronting their differences, becomes a coherent demand required by an assumed unfinishedness that reveals itself as ethical. For this reason the lack of respect or even the denial of this ethical basis of our unfinishedness cannot be regarded as anything other than a "rupture" with "right thinking." What I'm saying is that whoever wants to become a macho, a racist, or a hater of the lower classes, may of course do so. But I do not accept that this choice does not constitute a transgression of our essential humanity. It's of no use coming to me with arguments justifying genetically, sociologically, historically, or philosophically the superiority of whites over blacks, men over women, bosses over workers. All discrimination is immoral, and to struggle against it is a duty whatever the conditionings that have to be confronted. In fact, it is in this very struggle and duty that the charm, even the beauty, of our humanity resides. To know that I must respect the autonomy and the identity of the student demands the kind of practice that is coherent with this knowledge.

Common Sense

It is important to be constantly vigilant and rigorously evaluate any practice in the light of common sense. But even without such thorough reflection, simple good sense dictates that the sort of insensitive formalism in carrying out my duty as a teacher that would lead me to refuse a student's homework, even when accompanied by convenient explanations, constitutes a negative attitude on my part. It is my good sense that will tell me that exercising my authority in the classroom through the decisions I make, the activities I direct, the tasks I assign, and the goals I set for both individuals and the group is not a sign of authoritarianism. It seems that we have not yet solved the dilemma arising from the tension between authority and freedom. And we invariably confuse authority and authoritarianism, freedom and license.

I don't need a teacher of ethics to tell me that my pointed criticism of a postgraduate thesis would be unacceptable if another examiner had exceeded him/herself in severity. Should one of the examiners act in such a way, even if I happen to agree with the content of the argument, I could have no option but to publicly sympathize with the student and share with him or her the pain of such exaggerated criticism.[3] I don't need a professor of ethics to tell me that. My good sense is sufficient.

To know that I must respect the autonomy, the dignity, and the identity of the student and, in practice, must try to develop coherent attitudes and virtues in regard to such practice is an essential requirement of my profession, unless I am to become an empty mouther of words.[4] It serves no purpose, except to irritate and demoralize the student, for me to talk of democracy and freedom and at the same time act with the arrogance of a know-all.

The exercise of good sense, which can only add to our stature, belongs inherently to the "body" of curiosity. In this sense the more we practice methodically our capacity to question, to compare, to doubt, and to weigh, the more efficaciously curious we become and the more attuned becomes our good sense. The exercise or the education of our good sense will consequently overcome, by degrees, the merely instinctual elements in it, by means of which we frequently judge events in which we are involved. In addition, if in the context of a moral assessment that I make regarding some issue, I see that good sense is not enough to orient or ground my tactics for any given struggle, it can nevertheless still have a fundamental role in my evaluation of the scene, with the ethical implications that are integral to it.

My good sense will tell me, for example, that it is immoral to affirm that the hunger and misery that afflicts millions of Brazilians and millions of others worldwide is an immutable destiny in the face of which all we can do is to wait patiently for change to come. Far from being immutable, such a calamity—caused in great part by the greed of an insatiable minority—can be challenged. I can affirm, for example, with scientific rigor that a key element in changing this situation is an appeal to simple and disciplined rationality.

My good sense tells me that there is something to be learned from the fearful, faraway silence of Peter, hiding from himself. It will tell me that the problem is not so much related to the irrepressible energy, the tumult, the vitality of the other children. It may not tell me exactly what I want to know, but it will tell me that there is something I must know. In this case, good sense leads into critical epistemology, without which good sense is likely to lead to erroneous conclusions. However, critical epistemology without good sense, without the capacity to "divine," to follow a hunch, to be open to doubt, to be humble enough to know that one can err, is a recipe for failure. I feel pity and sometimes fear for the researcher who exhibits undue confidence in his/her certainty—an author of truth. And who is unable to recognize the historicity of his/her own knowledge.

It's my good sense in the first place that leads me to suspect that the school, which is the space in which both teachers and students are the subjects of education, cannot abstract itself from the sociocultural and economic conditions of its students, their families, and their communities.

It's impossible to talk of respect for students for the dignity that is in the process of coming to be, for the identities that are in the process of construction, without taking into consideration the conditions in which they are living and the importance of the knowledge derived from life experience, which they bring with them to school. I can in no way underestimate such knowledge. Or what is worse, ridicule it.

The more my own practice as a teacher increases in methodological rigor, the more respect I must have for the ingenuous knowledge of the student. For this ingenuous knowledge is the starting point from which his/her epistemological curiosity will work to produce a more critically scientific knowledge.

Reflecting on the duty I have as a teacher to respect the dignity, autonomy, and identity of the student, all of which are in process of becoming, I ought to think also about how I can develop an educational practice in which that respect, which I know I owe to the student, can come to fruition instead of being simply neglected and denied. Such an educational practice will demand of me permanent critical vigilance in regard to the students. The ideal, of course, is that, sooner or later, some mechanism whereby the students can participate in such an evaluation should be worked out, because the teacher's work is not simply "with" him- or herself but makes sense only in the context of the teacher-student relationship.

This critical evaluation of one's practice reveals the necessity for a series of attitudes or virtues without which no true evaluation or true respect for the student can exist.

These attitudes or virtues—absolutely indispensable for putting into practice the kind of knowledge that leads to respect for the autonomy, dignity, and identity of the student—are the result of a constructive effort that we impose on ourselves so as to diminish the distance between what we say and what we do. In fact, this diminution of the distance between discourse and practice constitutes an indispensable virtue, namely that of coherence. How, for example, can I continue to speak of respect for the dignity of the student if I discriminate, inhibit, or speak ironically from the height of my own arrogance, if the testimony that I give is that of an irresponsible omission of duty in the preparation and organization of my practice, in the question of rights, in denouncing injustices?[5] The exercise of the art and practice of teaching (a specifically human art), is of itself profoundly formational and, for that reason, ethical. True, those who exercise this art and practice do not have to be saints or angels. But they ought to have integrity and a clear sense of what is right and just.

The teacher's responsibility is considerable, though often we are not aware of it. The formational nature of this art and practice tells us already how the teacher should exercise this responsibility. For example, his/her presence in the classroom never escapes the student's judgments. The worst of which could be to conclude that the teacher's presence is an "absence."

Whether the teacher is authoritarian, undisciplined, competent, incompetent, serious, irresponsible, involved, a lover of people and of life, cold, angry with the world, bureaucratic, excessively rational, or whatever else, he/she will not pass through the classroom without leaving his or her mark on the students. Hence, the importance of the example the teacher shows in terms of clarity in regard to the task and in terms of his/her capacity in regard to both rights and duties. The teacher has the duty to give classes, to perform his/her teaching role. And to fulfill this duty, certain conditions are necessary: hygiene, proper physical space, an aesthetic environment. Without these "spaces," pedagogical "space" will suffer. At times, the lack of such spaces creates an environment in which it is pedagogically impossible to operate. And this constitutes an offense toward both educators and learners and to the art of teaching itself.

Humility, Tolerance, and the Struggle for the Rights of Educators

If there is something that Brazilian students should know from their earliest years, it is that respect for educators and for education itself includes the struggle for salaries that are worthy of the status of the teaching profession. And that this struggle is a matter of solemn duty. In this sense, the struggle of teachers' defense of their dignity and rights should be understood as an integral part of their teaching practice. Something that belongs essentially to the ethical basis of such practice and not something that comes from outside the activity of teaching. Something that is integral to it. The struggle to bring dignity to the practice of teaching is as much a part of the activity of teaching as is the respect that the teacher should have for the identity of the student, for the student himself or herself, and his or her right to be. One of the worst evils done to us in Brazil by the constituted authorities ever since the foundation of our society is to force us into a fatalistic and cynical indifference, born of existential weariness, caused by the almost complete abandonment in which they have left the educational system. "There is nothing we can do about it," is the tired refrain we often hear but that we cannot accept.

My respect as a teacher for the student, for his/her curiosity and fear that I ought not to curtail or inhibit by inappropriate gestures or attitudes, demands of me the cultivation of humility and tolerance. How can I respect the curiosity of the students if, lacking genuine humility and a convinced understanding of the role of the unknown in the process of reaching the known, I am afraid of revealing my own ignorance? How can I consider myself to be an educator, especially in the context of open-minded and enlightened teaching practice, if I cannot learn to live—whether it cost me little or much—with what is different? How can I be an educator if I do not develop in myself a caring and loving attitude toward the student, which is indispensable on the part of one who is committed to teaching and to the education process itself. I can only dislike what I am doing under the pain of not doing it well. I have no reason to exercise my teaching function badly. My response to the offense committed against education is to struggle conscientiously, critically, politically, and in a strategic manner against those who commit such an offense. I may even arrive at the state of weariness where I am tempted to abandon it in the search for something better. What I cannot do is remain in it and drag it down by a sense of frustration and lack of esteem toward myself and toward the students.

One of the forms of struggle against the lack of respect for education on the part of the constituted authorities is, on the one hand, our own refusal to transform our teaching into a mere sideline and, on the other hand, our rejection of a domesticating, paternal attitude toward the students.

It is in our seriousness as professional people with a competence for political organization that our strength as educators resides. This picture of our strength is really how we ought to see ourselves. It is in this sense that our teaching unions and other bodies ought to give priority to ongoing education among us as an important political task. And this political task will, obviously, bring up the question of the strike as an instrument of struggle. As something that may be, ought to be, rethought. Not that we will necessarily not use it any more. But given that it is a historically conditioned form of struggle, perhaps there is a need to look at new or reinvented forms.

Capacity to Apprehend Reality

Another kind of knowledge fundamental to educational practice is that which is linked to the very nature of this practice. As a teacher, I need to have clarity in regard to what I am engaged in. I need to know the various dimensions that are part of the essence of this practice, which can make me more secure in the way I approach it.

The best starting point for such reflections is the unfinishedness of our human condition. It is in this consciousness that the very possibility of learning, of being educated, resides. It is our immersion in this consciousness that gives rise to a permanent movement of searching, of curious interrogation that leads us not only to an awareness of the world but also to a thorough, scientific knowledge of it. This permanent movement of searching creates a capacity for learning not only in order to adapt to the world but especially to intervene, to re-create, and to transform it. All of this is evidence of our capacity for learning, for completing our incompleteness in a distinct way from that characteristic of other mammals or of plants.

Our capacity to learn, the source of our capacity to teach, suggests and implies that we also have a capacity to grasp the substantiveness/ essence of the object of our knowing. Mere mechanical memorization of the superficial aspects of the object is not true learning. Such a relationship with the object makes the learner into a kind of passive instrument who "transfers" some contents, but this so-called learning is a denial of critical epistemological curiosity, which is a participation in and a construction of knowledge of the object. It is precisely because of this capacity or skill for seizing the substantiveness of an object that we can take a negative learning experience, in which the learner was a mere passive receiver of a transference on the part of a teacher, and reconstruct it in terms of critical epistemological curiosity.

Women and men that we are, we are the only beings who have socio-historically developed the capacity for "seizing" substantively the object of our knowing. For that reason we are the only beings for whom learning is a creative adventure. Something much richer than the simple repetition of a lesson or of something already given. For us, to learn is to construct, to reconstruct, to observe with a view to changing—none of which can be done without being open to risk, to the adventure of the spirit.

I believe that I can state without equivocation, at this moment, that all educational practice requires the existence of "subjects," who while teaching, learn. And who in learning also teach. The reciprocal learning between teachers and students is what gives educational practice its gnostic character. It is a practice that involves the use of methods, techniques, materials; in its directive character, it implies objectives, dreams, utopias, ideas. Hence we have the political nature of education and the capacity that all educational practices have in being political and never neutral.

In being specifically human, education is gnostic and directive and for this reason, political. It is artistic and moral as it uses techniques as a means to facilitate teaching; it involves frustrations, fears, and desires. It requires of a teacher a general competence that involves knowledge of the nature of knowledge itself as well as the specific knowledges linked to one's field of specialization.

As a teacher who claims to have a progressive orientation and if I am coherent with that progressive posture, I cannot fall into a type of naiveté that will lead me to think that I am equal to my students. I cannot fail to know the specificity of my work as teacher and reject my fundamental role in positively contributing so that my students become actors in their own learning. If I work with children, I should be aware of the difficult transition or path from heteronomy to autonomy. I should always be alert that my presence and my work could either help or impede students in their own unquiet search for knowledge; if I work with youths or adults, I should not be any less attentive to what role my work may play in either motivating the students or sending them the message that there is something deeply wrong with them that needs fixing.

In essence, my position has to be of a person who wants or refuses to change. I cannot deny or hide my posture, but I also cannot deny others the right to reject it. In the name of the respect I should have toward my students, I do not see why I should omit or hide my political stance by proclaiming a neutral position that does not exist. On the contrary, my role as a teacher is to assent the students' right to compare, to choose, to rupture, to decide.

Recently, a young man who had begun his university studies told me, "I do not understand how you defend the rights of landless peasants who, in reality, are nothing but troublemakers." I responded that you do have some troublemakers among the landless peasants, but their struggle against oppression is both legitimate and ethical. The so-called troublemakers represent a form of resistance against those who aggressively oppose the agrarian reform. For me, the immorality and the lack of ethics rest with those who want to maintain an unjust order.

Our conversation went no further than that. The young man shook my hand in silence. I do not know how he dealt with our conversation afterward, but it is important that I said what I thought and that he heard from me that what I thought was right and should be said.

This is the road I have tried to follow as a teacher: living my convictions; being open to the process of knowing and sensitive to the experience of teaching as an art; being pushed forward by the challenges that prevent me from bureaucratizing my practice; accepting my limitations, yet always conscious of the necessary effort to overcome them and aware that I cannot hide them because to do so would be a failure to respect both my students and myself as a teacher.

Joy and Hope

Furthermore, my involvement with educational practice in its political, moral, and gnostic context has always been characterized by joy, which obviously does not mean that I have always been able to create it in my students. But I have never ceased to try to create a pedagogical space in which joy has its privileged role.

There is a relationship between the joy essential to teaching activity and hope. Hope is something shared between teachers and students. The hope that we can learn together, teach together, be curiously impatient together, produce something together, and resist together the obstacles that prevent the flowering of our joy. In truth, from the point of view of the human condition, hope is an essential component and not an intruder. It would be a serious contradiction of what we are if, aware of our unfinishedness, we were not disposed to participate in a constant movement of search, which in its very nature is an expression of hope. Hope is a natural, possible, and necessary impetus in the context of our unfinishedness. Hope is an indispensable seasoning in our human, historical experience. Without it, instead of history we would have pure determinism. History exists only where time is problematized and not simply a given. A future that is inexorable is a denial of history.

It needs to be clear that the absence of hope is not the "normal" way to be human. It is a distortion. I am not, for example, first of all a being without hope who may or may not later be converted to hope. On the contrary, I am first a being of hope who, for any number of reasons, may thereafter lose hope. For this reason, as human beings, one of our struggles should be to diminish the objective reasons for that hopelessness that immobilizes us.

In my view, it is therefore an enormous contradiction that an open-minded person who does not fear what is new, who is upset by injustice, who is hurt by discrimination, who struggles against impunity, and who refuses cynical and immobilizing fatalism should not be full of critical hope.

Recently in Olinda, one rainy yet sun-filled tropical morning, I was walking through a ghetto with Danilson Pinto, a young grassroots educator. Our conversation was something special, with Danilson revealing, with great fluidity of speech in almost every word and reflection that he emitted, the coherence with which he lived his democratic, grassroots convictions. In that environment of every kind of negation, both psychological and physical, in an environment of violence and the threat of violence and of despair, offense, and pain, in an environment where weaving the threads of life is possible only at the cost of courageous obstinacy, there we walked and talked with our hearts and minds curious and receptive, open to the world. As we walked through the streets of this place, hurt and offended by abandonment, I began to remember experiences of my youth in other ghettos of Olinda and Recife. Conversations with men and women whose souls seemed to have been torn by the cruelty of life. We seemed to be trampling on human sorrow as we talked about the different kinds of problems peculiar to this place. What can we possibly do, as educators, working in a context like this? Is there something we can do? And how can we do it? What do we as so-called educators need to know to be able to take the first steps in bringing together women, men, and children whose humanity has been betrayed and whose existence has been crushed? Prisoners without options, decisions, freedom, or ethics. "What can be done? The world is that way anyway," would become a standard response, as predictable, monotonous, and repetitive as human existence itself. In such a deterministic scenario, nothing new, nothing revolutionary, is possible.

I have a right to be angry, to show it and to use it as a motivational foundation for my struggle, just as I have a right to love and to express my love to the world and to use it as a motivational foundation for my struggle because I live in history at a time of possibility and not of determinism. If reality were pure determinism because it was thus decided or planned, there would be no reason at all to be angry. My right to be angry presupposes that the historical experience in which I participate tomorrow is not a given but a challenge and a problem. My just anger is grounded in any indignation in the face of the denial of the rights inherent in the very essence of the human condition. We stopped in the middle of a narrow footbridge that leads from the ghetto to a less neglected part of the town. We looked down on the bend of a polluted, lifeless river, more mud than water, where tufts of weeds suffocated in the stench. "Worse than the weeds," said Danilson, "is the waste ground of the public rubbish dump. The people who live in the area search among the rubbish for something to eat, for some garment to wear. This is how they survive." From this horrible dump, two years ago, a woman dug out the pieces of an amputated breast and cooked it for the family's Sunday dinner. The press got hold of the story and I also wrote about it in my recent book *Pedagogy of the Heart*. I do not know what reaction it provoked among pragmatic neoliberal thinkers, except perhaps the usual fatalistic shrug of the shoulders that says: "It's sad, but nothing can be done about it. That's the way things are."

Reality, however, is not inexorable or unchangeable. It happens to be this just as it could well be something else. And if we so-called progressive thinkers want it to be something else, we have to struggle. I confess that I would feel extremely sad, even desolated, and without any meaning for my presence in the world if there were strong and convincing reasons for saying that human existence is ultimately deterministic. I cannot, therefore, fold my arms fatalistically in the face of misery, thus evading my responsibility, hiding behind lukewarm, cynical shibboleths that justify my inaction because "there is nothing that can be done." The exhortation to be more a spectator; the invitation to (even exaltation of) silence, which in fact immobilizes those who are silenced; the hymn in praise of adaptability to fate or destiny; all these forms of discourse are negations of that humanization process for which we have an unshirkable responsibility.

Adaptability to situations that constitute a denial of humanization are acceptable only as a consequence of the experience of being dominated or enslaved or as a form of resistance or as a tactic in political struggle. I pretend that I accept the condition of being silenced now so as to fight, when the opportunity arises, against what constitutes a denial of my own humanity. This legitimization of anger in the face of a fatalistic acceptance of the negation of the process of humanization was a theme implicit in our conversation during all that morning.

Conviction That Change Is Possible

One of the first kinds of knowledge indispensable to the person who arrives in a ghetto or in a place marked by the betrayal of our right "to be" is the kind of knowledge that becomes solidarity, becomes a "being with." In that context, the future is seen not as inexorable but as something that is constructed by people engaged together in life, in history. It's the knowledge that sees history as possibility and not as already determined. The world is not finished. It is always in the process of becoming. The subjectivity with which I dialectically relate to the world, my role in the world, is not restricted to a process of only observing what happens but it also involves my intervention as a subject of what happens in the world. My role in the world is not simply that of someone who registers what occurs but of someone who has an input into what happens. I am equally subject and object in the historical process. In the context of history, culture, and politics, I register events not so as to adapt myself to them but so as to change them, in the physical world itself. I am not impotent. For example, our knowledge of earthquakes has helped us develop the kind of engineering that now makes it possible to survive earthquakes. We can't eliminate them, but we can minimize their effects. So, by our capacity to register facts and occurrences, we become capable of intervention. And this generates new kinds of knowledge far more complex than simple adaptation to a given and "unchangeable" situation. For this reason I do not accept (because it is not possible) the ingenuous or strategically neutral position often claimed by people in education or by those who study biology, physics, sociology, or mathematics. No one can be in the world, with the world, and with others and maintain a posture of neutrality. I cannot be in the world decontextualized, simply observing life. Yes, I can take up my position and settle myself, but only so as to become aware of my insertion into a context of decision, choice, and intervention. There are insistent questions that we all have to ask and that make it clear to us that it is not possible to study simply for the sake of studying. As if we could study in a way that really had nothing to do with that distant, strange world out there.

For what and for whom do I study? And against what and against whom? What meaning would Danilson's life and work have in that subworld of misery that we were walking through if some imperiously powerful force were to decree that those people had no option but to remain victims of the cruel necessity that has devastated their lives? The only thing he could possibly do would be to improve the people's capacity to adapt themselves to that inevitable negation of their existence. Thus, his practice could be no more than a hymn of praise to resignation. However, to the extent that the future is not inexorably sealed and already decided, there is another task that awaits us. Namely, the task of discussing the inherent openness of the future, making it as obvious as the misery that reigns in the ghetto. Also making it obvious that adaptability to suffering, hunger, disease, and the lack of hygiene, experienced intimately by each one, can be a strategy not just of physical but also of cultural resistance. It is resistance to the abusive abandonment in which the poor have to live. Essentially, both these aspects of resistance are strategies necessary for the physical and cultural survival of the oppressed. Afro-Brazilian religious syncretism is one example of how African culture in the context of slavery defended itself against the domination of the white colonizer.

It's necessary then, for us to have the kind of resistance that keeps us alive. It is also necessary that we know how to resist so as to remain alive, that our comprehension of the future is not static but dynamic, and that we are convinced that our vocation for greatness and not mediocrity is an essential expression of the process of humanization in which we are inserted. These are the bases for our nonconformity, for our refusal of that destructive resignation in the face of oppression. It is not by resignation but by a capacity for indignation in the face of injustice that we are affirmed.

One of the basic questions that we need to look at is how to convert merely rebellious attitudes into revolutionary ones in the process of the radical transformation of society. Merely rebellious attitudes or actions are insufficient, though they are an indispensable response to legitimate anger. It is necessary to go beyond rebellious attitudes to a more radically critical and revolutionary position, which is in fact a position not simply of denouncing injustice but of announcing a new utopia. Transformation of the world implies a dialectic between the two actions: denouncing the process of dehumanization and announcing the dream of a new society.

On the basis of this knowledge, namely, "to change things is difficult but possible," we can plan our political-pedagogical strategy. It is of no importance whether our commitment be in the area of adult or child literacy, health, evangelization, or the inculcation of new technical skills.

The success of Danilson and educators like him derives from the certainty that it is possible to change and necessary to change. For it is clear to them that allowing concrete situations of misery to persist is immoral. Thus, this type of knowledge that the historical process unfolds leads into a principle of action, thus opening the way in practice to the contribution of other kinds of indispensable knowledge.

Obviously, it is not a question of inciting the exploited poor to rebellion, to mobilization, to organization, to shaking up the world. In truth, it's a question of working in some given area, be it literacy, health, or evangelization, and doing so as to awake the conscience of each group, in a constructive, critical manner, about the violence and extreme injustice of this concrete situation. Even further, to make it clear that this situation is not the immutable will of God.

I cannot accept the philosophy or the tactics of those who believe that the worse the situation is, the better. At the same time, I reject categorically realpolitik, which simply anesthetize the oppressed and postpone indefinitely the necessary transformations in society. I cannot stop the oppressed, with whom I may be working in a ghetto, from voting for reactionary politicians, but I have the duty to warn them of the error they are committing—of the contradiction they are involving themselves in. To vote for a reactionary politician is to guarantee the preservation of the status quo. If I consider myself to be coherently progressive, how can I vote for a politician whose rhetoric is an affront to solidarity and an apology for racism?

If I take as a starting point that the condition of misery in which the oppressed live is first and foremost a condition of violence and not an expression of the will of a punitive God, nor the fruit of laziness or miscegenation, then as an educator my task is to become ever more capable and skilled. If I do not, then my struggle loses its efficacy. What I am saying is that the kind of knowledge I have just spoken of, namely, "to change is difficult but possible," the kind of knowledge that gives me hope and spurs me into action, is not sufficient for the kind of efficacy I referred to above. Firmly rooted in such knowledge, I must at the same time review other specific kinds of knowledge in which my practice is based and that nourish my curiosity. How, for example, can I hope to engage in literacy without precise knowledge about the acquisition of skills in the area of teaching how to read and write? On the other hand, how can I work in any field, whether it be in literacy, in production, in cooperatives, in evangelization, in health, without at the same time acquiring a knowledge of the skills and crafts, even the astuteness, with which human groups produce their own survival?

As an educator I need to be constantly "reading" the world inhabited by the grassroots with which I work, that world that is their immediate context and the wider world of which they are part. What I mean is that on no account may I make little of or ignore in my contact with such groups the knowledge they acquire from direct experience and out of which they live. Or their way of explaining the world, which involves their comprehension of their role and presence in it. These knowledges are explicit, suggested, or hidden in what I call the decoding of the world, which in its turn always precedes the decoding of the word.

If, on the one hand, I am unable to adapt myself or be "converted" to the way of thinking (ingenuous knowledge) of grassroots groups, on the other hand, I cannot insofar as I consider myself to be progressive, impose in an arrogant fashion, the "truth" of my way of thinking. Through dialogue, grassroots groups can be challenged to process their social-historical experience as the experience that is formative for them individually and collectively. And through such dialogue the necessity of going beyond certain types of explanations of the "facts" will become obvious.

One of the most objectionable errors of political militants, especially those of the messianically authoritarian kind, has always been a total ignorance of grassroots comprehension of the world. Seeing themselves as bearers of the "truth" that no one can refuse, they regard their sublime task as one not of proposing such truth for consideration but of imposing it without question.

Recently I heard a debate in which a young working man, speaking of life in a ghetto, said that he no longer felt shame because of where he lived. "I am proud," he said, "of what we have achieved through our struggle and our organization. In fact, if we really had a clear awareness of our condition and its structural causes, we would see that it is not we who should be ashamed of where we live but those who live in comfort but do nothing to change the misery that surrounds them."

It's possible that this young man's statement produced little or no reaction in the minds of any authoritarian or messianic militant. One could imagine some negative reaction from someone more in love with revolutionary ideas than actually committed to them. In essence, the way the young man talked was a demonstration of how he was able to "read" his world and his own experience in it. If in the past he was ashamed, now he was capable of perceiving that the condition in which he found himself was not of his making. And especially, he had learned that that situation was not unchangeable. His struggle was much more important in bringing about his new awareness than the rantings of any sectarian, messianically obsessed militant. It's important to stress that the breakthrough of a new form of awareness in understanding the world is not the privilege of one person. The experience that makes possible the "breakthrough" is a "collective" experience. However, usually someone or another will, individually, put forward and explicate a new perception of this social reality. One of the fundamental tasks of the educator who is open-minded is to be attentive and sensitive to the way a given social group reads and re-reads its reality, so as to be able to stimulate progressively a generalized comprehension of this new reality.

It's important always to bear in mind that the role of the dominant ideology is to inculcate in the oppressed a sense of blame and culpability about their situation of oppression. And this sense of blame and culpability becomes transparent at certain times. A case in point is one I came across in a Catholic institution in California. A poor woman was telling me about her problems and difficulties, of how great an affliction she was suffering. I felt impotent. I did not know what to say. I felt indignation for what she was going through. In the end, I asked her: "Are you American?"

"No," she replied, "I am poor." It was as if what was uppermost in her mind was her sense of being a failure. And that that was her own fault. Something she almost had to ask pardon for from the society that she was part of, namely, North America. I can still see her blue eyes full of tears, tears of suffering and self-blame for having been a personal failure. People like her are part of a legion of wounded and marginalized who have not yet understood that the cause of their suffering is the perversity of the socio-political and economic system under which they live. As long as they think like this, they simply reinforce the power of this system. In fact, they connive, unconsciously, with a dehumanizing socio-political order.

For example, literacy circles introduced in poor areas only make sense in the context of the humanizing process. In other words, they should open up conjointly the possibility of a socio-historical and political equivalent of psychoanalysis whereby the sense of self-blame that has been falsely interjected can be cast out. This expulsion of self-blame corresponds to the expulsion of the invasive shadow of the oppressor that inhabits the psyche of the oppressed. Of course, once this shadow is expelled, it needs to be substituted in the oppressed by a sense of autonomy and responsibility.

It is worth noting, however, that in spite of the political and ethical relevance of the effort of conscientization that I have just spoken of, it is insufficient in itself. It is important to go on from there to the teaching of writing and reading the word. We cannot, in a democratic context, transform a literacy circle into either a campaign for political revolution or a space totally given over to an analysis of what is going on in our world. The essential task of those like Danilson, with whom I identify myself, is to try out, with conviction and passion, the dialectical relation between a reading of the world and a reading of the word.

If we reflect on the fact that our human condition is one of essential unfinishedness, that, as a consequence, we are incomplete in our being and in our knowing, then it becomes obvious that we are "programmed" to learn, destined by our very incompleteness to seek completeness, to have a "tomorrow" that adds to our "today." In other words, wherever there are men and women, there is always and inevitably something to be done, to be completed, to be taught, and to be learned.

In my opinion, none of this makes any sense if attempted outside the socio-historical context in which men and women find themselves and within which they discover their vocation to find "completeness," to become "more."

Teaching Requires Curiosity

To me, the epitome of negation in the context of education is the stifling or inhibition of curiosity in the learner and, consequently, in the teacher too. In other words, the educator who is dominated by authoritarian or paternalistic attitudes that suffocate the curiosity of the learner finishes by suffocating his or her own curiosity. There is no possible ethical foundation for denying the expression of curiosity in the "other." A parent's curiosity that expresses itself in policing how and where the child's curiosity is going ends up becoming stale and withered. The curiosity that in essence tries to silence the other is, in fact, a denial of itself. A proper democratic and pedagogical environment in which to work is one in which the learners progress in learning through their actual experiences and one in which curiosity as an expression of freedom necessarily has limits, limits that are being constantly called into being. Limits that are ethically integrated by the learner. My curiosity does not have the right to invade the world of the other so as to expose that world to the scrutiny of all.

As a teacher, I ought to know that I can neither teach nor learn unless driven, disturbed, and forced to search by the energy that curiosity brings to my being. To exercise any curiosity correctly is a right that I have as a person and to which there corresponds a responsibility to struggle in defense of this right. If my curiosity is domesticated, I may obtain a level of mechanical memorization of certain aspects of things but never a real grasp or an essential knowledge of the object. The construction or the production of knowledge of the object to be known implies the exercise of curiosity in its critical capacity to distance itself from the object, to observe it, to delimit it, to divide it up, to close in on it, to approach it methodically to make comparisons, to ask questions.

To stimulate questions and critical reflection about the questions, asking what is meant by this or that question, is fundamental to curiosity. Otherwise, all we have is the passivity of students in the face of the discursive explanations of the teacher and answers to questions that have not been asked. This does not mean, of course, that we ought to reduce our teaching activity to the simple to-and-fro questions that may also become tedious and sterile, all in the name of defending the necessity of curiosity. The need for dialogue does not in any way diminish the need for explanation and exposition whereby the teacher sets forth his/her understanding and knowledge of the object. What is really essential in this process is that both the teacher and the students know that open, curious questioning, whether in speaking or listening, is what grounds them mutually— not a simple passive pretense at dialogue. The important thing is for both teacher and students to assume their epistemological curiosity.

In this sense, the good teacher is the one who manages to draw the student into the intimacy of his or her thought process while speaking. The class then becomes a challenge and not simply a nest where people gather. In the environment of challenge, the students become tired but they do not fall asleep. They get tired because they accompany the comings and goings of the teacher's thought and open their eyes in wonder at his or her pauses, doubts, uncertainties.

Even before attempting to discuss methods and tactics for the purpose of creating dynamic classes like these, the teacher must be clear and content with the notion that the cornerstone of the whole process is human curiosity. Curiosity is what makes me question, know, act, ask again, recognize.

It would be an excellent weekend task to propose to a group of students that each one single out the most striking curiosity he or she has experienced, connected with TV news propaganda, a videogame, a gesture of someone they know—any circumstance at all. It does not matter. What type of response did they make to their curiosity? Was it easily forgotten, or did it lead to other curiosities? Did this process involve a consultation of sources, the using of dictionaries, computers, books, or other people? Did this curiosity constitute a challenge, a provocation for some provisional knowledge, or did it not? What did one person feel when she/he discovered someone else working on the same curiosity? Finally, the students should consider the question of whether or not a person can be curious if prepared to think about his/her own curiosity.

The experience could be refined and deepened to the point, for example, where a seminar could be organized on a twice-weekly basis so as to debate the various types of curiosity and their implications and consequences.

The exercise of curiosity makes it more critically curious, more methodically rigorous in regard to its object. The more spontaneous curiosity intensifies and becomes rigorous, the more epistemological it becomes.

I've never been an ingenuous lover of technology; I do not deify it nor demonize it. For that reason I've always felt at ease in dealing with it. I've no doubt about the enormous potential for technology to motivate and challenge children and adolescents of the less-favored social classes. For that reason alone, as secretary of education for the city of São Paulo, I introduced the computer to the city's schools. In fact, my grandchildren are able to tell me about their curiosity and how it has been inspired by the computer, which for them is a normal part of living.

The exercise of curiosity convokes the imagination, the emotions, and the capacity to conjecture and to compare in tracing a profile of the object to be known as well as its raison d'être. A sound, for example, may provoke my curiosity. It focuses on the space where I think it is happening. I sharpen my ear. I compare it to other sounds that I already know. I investigate the space a little closer. I develop several hypotheses about the possible origin of the sound. Then, by process of elimination, I arrive at a satisfactory explanation.

Having satisfied one curiosity, a further search continues. There could be no such thing as human existence without the openness of our being to the world, without the transitiveness of our consciousness.

The more skill and methodological rigor I acquire in handling these various operations, the greater will be the exactitude with which I approach the objects of my curiosity.

One of the fundamental types of knowledge in my critical-educative practice is that which stresses the need for spontaneous curiosity to develop into epistemological curiosity.

Another indispensable type of knowledge in this field is that which enables us to handle the relationship between authority and freedom, which is an area of permanent tension between discipline and undiscipline.[6]

Resulting from the harmony between authority and freedom, discipline necessarily implies respect of the one for the other. And this respect is expressed in the admission that both make regarding the limits that cannot be transgressed on either side.

Authoritarianism and freedom with no boundaries are ruptures in the tense harmony between authority and freedom. Authoritarianism is the rupture in favor of authority against freedom. And unbridled freedom is the rupture in favor of freedom against authority. Both authoritarianism and freedom with no bounds are undisciplined forms of behavior that deny what I am calling the ontological vocation of the human being.[7]

So, as there is no room for discipline either in authoritarianism or in unbridled freedom, both lack rigor, authority, and freedom. Only in those practices where authority and freedom are found and preserved in their autonomy (that is, in a relationship of mutual respect) can we speak of a disciplined practice as well as a practice favorable to the vocation "to be more."

Here in Brazil, our authoritarian past is now being challenged by an ambiguous modernity, with the result that we oscillate between authoritarianism and boundless freedom. Between two types of tyranny: the tyranny of freedom and the tyranny of exacerbated authority. And sometimes, we experience the two simultaneously.

A really good exercise would be to explore the tension involved in the confrontation between authority and freedom. With such an exercise, one could evaluate the degree to which these opposites, in becoming themselves, remain autonomous in situations of dialogue. For this exercise to be possible, it is indispensable that both contrary concepts, authority and freedom, become increasingly convinced of the ideal of mutual respect as the only road to authenticity.

Let us begin by reflecting on a few of the qualities that democratic authority in teaching needs to incorporate in its relationship with the freedom of the students. It is interesting to note that my learning experience will be fundamental to the teaching I will be doing in the future or that I may happen to be doing now. It is in living critically my freedom as a learner that, in large part, I will prepare my authority as a teacher in the future or recover it in the present. To this end, as a student who dreams of becoming a teacher tomorrow or who is already teaching, I ought to have as the object of my curiosity the experiences I have lived with various teachers, as well as my own experiences with my own students. What I want to say is the following: I must not think only of the programmatic contents that are the themes of our discussions in the various teaching departments. I must reflect at the same time on the question of whether this or that teacher teaches in an open, dialogical way or in a closed, authoritarian way.

FOUR

TEACHING IS A HUMAN ACT

Is my curiosity able to express itself? Is it growing? In my opinion, one of the essential qualities that an authoritative, democratic teaching practice ought to reveal in its relationship with the freedom of students is a sense of its own self-confidence. It's a self-confidence that expresses itself in a firmness of action or of decision in regard to its respect for the freedom and autonomy of students, its ability to discuss its own positions, and its openness to reviewing both itself and its previously held positions.

If the teacher is imbued with self-confident authority, there will be no need for a speech about it at every available instant. If there is self-confidence regarding its legitimacy, there will be no need to ask anyone: "Do you know to whom you are speaking?"

Self-Confidence, Professional Competence, and Generosity

The self-confident authority with which the teacher is imbued implies another type of self-confidence that's grounded in professional competence. There is no such thing as teaching authority without this competence. Teachers who do not take their own education seriously, who do not study, who make little effort to keep abreast of events have no moral authority to coordinate the activities of the classroom. This does not mean of course that the teacher's choice and his or her democratic practice are determined by scientific competence.

There are teachers who are scientifically prepared but extremely authoritarian in practice. What I'm saying here is that professional incompetence destroys the legitimate authority of the teacher.

Another quality that is indispensable to genuine authority in the context of freedom in the classroom is generosity. The power of genuine authority to form students is emasculated and rendered impotent by small-mindedness, just as it is also impoverished by pharisaical or conceited arrogance. By an arrogance that is indulgent toward itself and toward those who belong to its circle. Such arrogance is a denial of generosity and of humility, for neither of these qualities rejoices in giving offense or in seeing someone humiliated. The climate of respect that is born of just, serious, humble, and generous relationships, in which both the authority of the teacher and the freedom of the students are ethically grounded, is what converts pedagogical space into authentic educational experience.

There is also a certain kind of greed, an almost unbridled lust for giving orders, that creates negative reactions and a totally incompatible climate for the exercise of true authority. This kind of rigid giving of orders elicits no creativity at all from the student. It does not consider the student as having a taste for adventure.

Coherently democratic authority, founded on the certainty and on the importance both of itself and of the freedom of the students, will never minimize freedom and yet will be dedicated to the construction of genuine discipline. Freedom is a must, a constant challenge. Genuine freedom, even rebellious freedom, in this context is never seen as a deterioration of order. Coherently democratic authority carries the conviction that true discipline does not exist in the muteness of those who have been silenced but in the stirrings of those who have been challenged, in the doubt of those who have been prodded, and in the hopes of those who have been awakened. Whatever I do or am involved in, whether it is pedagogy, biology, or astronomy, whether it is working the land or sailing, I am first and foremost a person. I know there is much that I do not know. And I also know that there is much that I know. For this reason, it is possible for me to know of what I do not yet know, as it is possible for me to know better what I actually know. And I will know better and more authentically what I know the more efficaciously I build up my autonomy vis-à-vis the autonomy of others.

There are two tasks I have never dichotomized. One is to make it always obvious to the students that respect for them is fundamental. The other is to respect myself. I have never been able to separate the teaching of contents from the ethical education of the students, as if they were disconnected moments. Even more so, coherent democratic authority recognizes the ethical basis of our presence in the world and necessarily recognizes that it is not possible to live ethically without freedom and that there is no such thing as freedom without risk. Teachers who exercise their freedom will feel that it becomes greater and more integrated to the degree that they ethically assume responsibility for their actions. To decide is to break with something, and, to do this, I have to run a risk. Hardly the kind of thing I am likely to do while sipping orange juice on a tropical beach. Even so, coherently democratic authority does not usually sin by omission. On the one hand, it refuses to silence the freedom of the students, and on the other hand, it rejects any inhibition of the process of constructing good discipline.

At the heart of the experience of coherently democratic authority is a basic, almost obsessive dream: namely, to persuade or convince freedom of its vocation to autonomy as it travels the road of self-construction, using materials from within and without, but elaborated over and over again. It is with this autonomy, laboriously constructed, that freedom will gradually occupy those spaces previously inhabited by dependency.

I cannot be a teacher without exposing who I am. Without revealing, either reluctantly or with simplicity, the way I relate to the world, how I think politically. I cannot escape being evaluated by the students, and the way they evaluate me is of significance for my modus operandi as a teacher. As a consequence, one of my major preoccupations is the approximation between what I say and what I do, between what I seem to be and what I am actually becoming.

If a student asks me the meaning of "distancing oneself epistemologically from the object," and I reply that I do not know but that I hope to be able to discover its meaning, my reply is one that, though it does not confer on me the authority of one who knows, does give me the joy of recognizing my ignorance and not needing to lie. And this commitment to the truth of my ignorance opens up a credit with the students that I ought to preserve. To have given a false answer, a jumble of words to cover up my ignorance, would be ethically impossible. However, precisely because my understanding and teaching practice puts me in a position of stimulating all types of questions, I need to be well prepared both to continue to be truthful with the students and to not have to continuously affirm that I do not know. Teaching practice, which doesn't exist unless there is learning simultaneously, is a holistic practice. The teaching of contents implies that the teacher be also grounded ethically. The beauty of the practice of teaching is made up of a passion for integrity that unites teacher and student. A passion that has roots in ethical responsibility. This is a beauty not sullied by superficiality or by coarse or pharisaical posturing. It is a beauty that is pure without being puritanical.

Here we are engaged in an effort to overcome debilitating dualisms because we are talking about the impossibility of separating the teaching of contents from ethical formation. Of separating practice and theory, authority and freedom, ignorance and knowledge, respect for the teacher and respect for the students, and teaching and learning. None of these terms can be mechanically separated one from the other. As a teacher, I am dealing with the exercise of my own freedom and my own authority. But I am at the same time dealing directly with the freedom of the students and the development of their autonomy, not forgetting that they are also in the process of building up their own authority. As a teacher, I cannot help the students to overcome their ignorance if I am not engaged permanently in trying to overcome my own. I cannot teach what I do not know. However, I am not referring here to effort and knowledge based on "words." I am talking about the way I live with my students. Because that is the most convincing argument. It is in my concrete respect for the right to question, to doubt, and to criticize that I bear witness to what I believe and speak. Simply speaking will never be enough.

The more I reflect on our educational practice, recognizing the responsibility it demands of us, the more I am convinced of our duty to struggle to make it respected. The respect that we as teachers owe to our students will not be easy to sustain in the absence of the dignity and the respect due to us on the part of public or private education authorities.

Commitment

Another type of knowledge that I ought to possess and that has to do with almost all of the others that I have so far spoken of is the understanding that the exercise of my teaching activity does not leave me untouched. No more than I could be out in the rain with no protection and expect not to get wet. We must understand the meaning of a moment of silence, of a smile, or even of an instance in which someone needs to leave the room. Or the fact that a question was asked perhaps a little discourteously. After all, our teaching space is a text that has to be constantly read, interpreted, written, and rewritten. In this sense, the more solidarity there is between teacher and student in the way this space is mutually used, the more possibilities for democratic learning will be opened up in the school.

It is my belief that today the progressive kind of teacher needs to watch out as never before for the clever uses of the dominant ideology of our time, especially its insidious capacity for spreading the idea that it is possible for education to be neutral. This is an extremely reactionary philosophy, which uses the classroom to inculcate in the students political attitudes and practices, as if it were possible to exist as a human being in the world and at the same time be neutral.

My very presence in the school as a teacher is intrinsically a political presence, something that students cannot possibly ignore. In this sense, I ought to transmit to the students my capacity to analyze, to compare, to evaluate, to decide, to opt, to break with. My capacity to be just, to practice justice, and to have a political presence. And as a presence, I cannot sin by omission. I am, by definition, a subject "destined" to choose. To have options. I honor truth. And all that means being ethical. It may help me or hinder me as a teacher, to know that I cannot escape the attention and evaluation of the students. Even so, it ought to make me aware of the care I need to take in carrying out my teaching activity. If I have made a choice for open-minded, democratic practice, then obviously this excludes reactionary, authoritarian, elitist attitudes and actions. Under no circumstances, therefore, may I discriminate against a student. In addition, the perception the student has of my teaching is not exclusively the result of how I act but also of how the student understands my action. Obviously, I cannot spend my life as a teacher asking the students what they think of me and my teaching activity. Even so, I ought to be attentive to their reading of my activity and interaction with them. Furthermore, we need to learn the significance of being ethical. It becomes a way of life.

Education as a Form of Intervention in the World

Another kind of knowledge whose existence I cannot doubt for a moment in my critical educative practice is that education, as a specifically human experience, is a form of intervention in the world. In addition to contents either well or badly taught, this type of intervention also implies both the reproduction of the dominant ideology and its unmasking. The dialectical nature of the educational process does not allow it to be only one or the other of these things.

Education never was, is not, and never can be neutral or indifferent in regard to the reproduction of the dominant ideology or the interrogation of it. It is a fundamental error to state that education is simply an instrument for the reproduction of the dominant ideology, as it is an error to consider it no more than an instrument for unmasking that ideology, as if such a task were something that could be accomplished simplistically, fundamentally, without obstacles and difficult struggles. These attitudes are serious errors, and they indicate a defective vision of both history and consciousness. On the one hand, we have a mechanistic comprehension of history that reduces consciousness to a simple reflex of matter, and on the other, we have a subjective idealism that tries to make the role of consciousness fit into the facts of history. As women and men, we are not simply determined by facts and events. At the same time, we are subject to genetic, cultural, social, class, sexual, and historical conditionings that mark us profoundly and that constitute for us a center of reference.

From the perspective of the dominant classes, there is no doubt of course that educational practice ought to cover up the truth and immobilize the classes. Conversely, these same interests are capable of being "progressive" when it suits them. Progressive by half, so to speak. They are able to bring into being technical advances that are understood and often carried out in a "neutral" way. It would be extremely naive on our part to believe that the ranchers' lobby would agree that our schools, both rural and urban, should discuss the questions of agrarian reform as an economic, political, and ethical problem of the greatest importance for the development of the country.

This task falls to progressive-minded educators, both inside and outside the schools. It's a task also for nongovernmental organizations and democratic-minded unions. On the one hand, we might expect modern-minded business with urban roots to be sympathetic to the cause of agrarian reform, because its interests in the expansion of the market seem "progressive" in the face of rural conservatism. On the other hand, the "progressiveness" of modern business, welcome as it is in contrast to the retrograde truculence of the ranchers, does not have to think twice about where its loyalty lies when confronted with a clash between human interests and the interests of the market.

I continue to ponder Marx's observation about the necessary radicality that enables me to be permanently aware of everything that has to do with the defense of human interests, which are superior to those of particular groups or classes of people.

Recognizing that precisely because we are constantly in the process of becoming and, therefore, are capable of observing, comparing, evaluating, choosing, deciding, intervening, breaking with, and making options, we are ethical beings, capable of transgressing our ethical grounding. However, though transgression of this grounding exists as a possibility, we can never claim transgression as a right. And, of course, we cannot sit idly by and fold our arms in the face of such a possibility. Hence my categorical refusal of fatalistic quietude, which, instead of condemning ethical transgression, tries to absorb it as if it belonged to "right" thinking. I cannot be complicit with a perverse system, exempting it from responsibility for its malice, by attributing to "blind forces" the damage caused to human beings.

Of course (and I restate my belief), modern business leaders accept, stimulate, and support technical training courses for their workers. What they obviously refuse is an education that both includes technical and scientific preparation and speaks of the workers' presence in the world. A human and ethical presence, debased every time it is transformed into pure shadow.

I cannot be a teacher if I do not perceive with ever greater clarity that my practice demands of me a definition about where I stand. A break with what is not right ethically. I must choose between one thing and another thing. I cannot be a teacher and be in favor of everyone and everything. I cannot be in favor merely of people, humanity, vague phrases far from the concrete nature of educative practice. Mass hunger and unemployment, side by side with opulence, are not the result of destiny, as certain reactionary circles would have us believe, claiming that people suffer because they can do nothing about the situation. The question here is not "destiny." It is immorality. Here I want to repeat—forcefully—that nothing can justify the degradation of human beings. Nothing. The advance of science or technology cannot legitimate "class" and call it "order" so that a minority who holds power may use and squander the fruits of the earth while the vast majority are hard pressed even to survive and often justify their own misery as the will of God. I refuse to add my voice to that of the "peacemakers" who call upon the wretched of the earth to be resigned to their fate. My voice is in tune with a different language, another kind of music. It speaks of resistance, indignation, the just anger of those who are deceived and betrayed. It speaks, too, of their right to rebel against the ethical transgressions of which they are the long-suffering victims.

The fatalistic philosophy of neoliberal politics of which I have been speaking is a case in point of how human interests are abandoned whenever they threaten the values of the market.

I cannot imagine, for example, a modern manager allowing one of his workers the right to discuss, during a literacy class or during an in-service training course in the factory, the pros and cons of the dominant ideology. For example, to discuss the question "unemployment today is an end-of-the-century inevitability." And, in that context, to ask: Why is agrarian reform not also an inevitability? And why not make putting an end to hunger and misery inevitable as well?

It's extremely reactionary to say that what only interests workers is achieving the highest grade of technical efficiency and that they do not want to get involved in ideological debates that, in any case, lead nowhere. It is in the context of the work situation that the worker needs to engage in the process of becoming a citizen, something that does not happen as a consequence of "technical efficiency." It is the result of a political struggle to re-creation of a kind of society that is both humane and just.

Thus, since I cannot be a teacher without considering myself prepared to teach well and correctly the contents of my discipline, I cannot reduce my teaching practice to the mere transmission of these contents. It is my ethical posture in the course of teaching these contents that will make the difference. It is a posture made up of my commitment to thoroughness, my investment in excellence, and my competent preparation that reveals humility rather than arrogance. It is a posture of unconditional respect for the students, for the knowledge they have that comes directly from life and that, together with the students, I will work to go beyond. My coherence in the classroom is as important as my teaching of contents. A coherence of what I say, write, and do.

I am a teacher who stands up for what is right against what is indecent, who is in favor of freedom against authoritarianism, who is a supporter of authority against freedom with no limits, and who is a defender of democracy against the dictatorship of right or left. I am a teacher who favors the permanent struggle against every form of bigotry and against the economic domination of individuals and social classes. I am a teacher who rejects the present system of capitalism, responsible for the aberration of misery in the midst of plenty. I am a teacher full of the spirit of hope, in spite of all signs to the contrary. I am a teacher who refuses the disillusionment that consumes and immobilizes. I am a teacher proud of the beauty of my teaching practice, a fragile beauty that may disappear if I do not care for the struggle and knowledge that I ought to teach. If I do not struggle for the material conditions without which my body will suffer from neglect, thus running the risk of becoming frustrated and ineffective, then I will no longer be the witness that I ought to be, no longer the tenacious fighter who may tire but who never gives up. This is a beauty that needs to be marveled at but that can easily slip away from me through arrogance or disdain toward my students.

It's important that students perceive the teacher's struggle to be coherent. And it is necessary that this struggle be the subject of discussion in the classroom from time to time. There are situations in which the teacher's attitude or practice may appear contradictory to the students. This apparent contradiction usually occurs when the teacher simply exercises authority in coordinating the activities of the class in a way that seems to the students an excess of power. At times it may be the teacher who is uncertain whether she or he overstepped the limits of authority or not.

Freedom and Authority

In another part of this text, I referred to the fact that we have not yet resolved the problem of tension between authority and freedom. Because we were dedicated to overcoming the legacy of authoritarianism so prevalent among us, we fell into the opposite error of limitless freedom, accusing the legitimate exercise of authority of being an abuse of authority.

Recently, a young university professor with democratic principles was telling me about what seemed to him an abuse in his way of handling authority. He told me, with a certain air of affliction, that he reacted to the presence of a student from another class who was standing at the half-open door gesticulating to one of the students of his class. In fact, he had to interrupt his teaching because of the disturbance. In so doing, he managed to focus attention on what was central, namely, his teaching activity and the climate necessary for its proper execution, to say nothing of his right and that of his students not to be interrupted by a clearly unacceptable expression of freedom without limits. Even so, he thought his decision had been arbitrary. Not so, in my view. In fact, not to have intervened would have amounted to a demonstration of a lack of real authority, an act of omission in the face of a clearly unacceptable and prejudicial intrusion into his teaching space.

In one of the many debates in which I have participated on the question of freedom and authority and the limits inherent in both (limits without which freedom is perverted into license and authority into authoritarianism), I heard one of the participants say that my "sing-song" reminded him of a reactionary teacher he had during the military regime. Freedom, according to my interlocutor, has no limits. It is above any and every limit. Obviously, I did not accept this position. Freedom without limit is as impossible as freedom that is suffocated or contracted. If it were without limit, it would take me outside of the sphere of human action, intervention, or struggle. Limitless freedom is a negation of the human condition of unfinishedness.

The great challenge for the democratic-minded educator is how to transmit a sense of limit that can be ethically integrated by freedom itself. The more consciously freedom assumes its necessary limits, the more authority it has, ethically speaking, to continue to struggle in its own name.

I would like to say once again how much I believe in freedom and how fundamental it is, in the exercise of freedom, to assume responsibility for our decisions. It was this kind of freedom that characterized my own experience as a son, a brother, a student, a teacher, a husband, and a citizen.

Freedom becomes mature in confrontation with other freedoms, defending its rights in relation to parental authority, the authority of teachers, and the authority of the state. It is clear, of course, that adolescents do not always makes the best decisions regarding their future. For that reason it is important for parents to take part in discussions about the future plans of their children. They cannot, ought not, deny that they must know and assume that the future of their children belongs to their children and not to the parents. In my view, it's preferable to emphasize the children's freedom to decide, even if they run the risk of making a mistake, than to simply follow the decision of the parents. It's in making decisions that we learn to decide. I can never learn to be who I am if I never decide anything because I always have the good sense and the wisdom of my mother and father to fall back on. The old arguments of "Imagine the risk you run and the time and opportunity wasted on this crazy idea," are simply invalid. What is pragmatic in our existence cannot be exalted above the ethical imperative that we must face. The child has, at the very least, the right to prove the craziness of his or her idea. However, it is essential to the learning experience of decision making that the consequences of any decision be assumed by the decision maker. There is no decision that is not followed by effects either expected, half expected, or not expected at all. Consequences are what make decision making a responsible process. One of the pedagogical tasks for parents is to make it clear to their children that parental participation in the decision-making process is not an intrusion but a duty, so long as the parents have no intention of deciding on behalf of their children. The participation of the parents is most opportune in helping the children analyze the possible consequences of the decision that is to be taken.

The position of the mother or father is that of someone who, without any risk to her or his authority, is able to accept, humbly, the extremely important role of adviser to a son or daughter. And as an adviser, will never impose a decision or become angry because the parental point of view was not accepted.

What is necessary, fundamentally, is that the son or daughter take on, responsibly and ethically, the weight of his or her own decision, which in fact amounts to a key moment in forging on the development of the individual's autonomy. No one is first autonomous and then makes a decision. Autonomy is the result of a process involving various and innumerable decisions. For example, why not challenge the child while still young to participate in a discussion and a decision about the best time to do schoolwork? Why is the best time for homework always the parent's time? Why waste the opportunity to emphasize the duty and the right that the children have, as people, to engage in the process of forging their own autonomy? No one is the subject of the autonomy of someone else. However, no one suddenly becomes mature at twenty-five years of age. Either we become mature with each day that passes or we do not. Autonomy is a process of becoming oneself, a process of maturing, of coming to be. It does not happen on a given date. In this sense, a pedagogy of autonomy should be centered on experiences that stimulate decision making and responsibility, in other words, on experiences that respect freedom.

One thing is very clear to me today. I have never been afraid of believing in freedom, in seriousness, in genuine love, in solidarity, or in the struggle in which I learned the value and importance of indignation. I have never been afraid of being criticized by my wife, by my children, or by the students with whom I have worked down the years because of my profound conviction of the value of freedom, hope, the word of another, and the desire of someone to try and try again as a result of having been more ingenuous than critical. What I have feared, at different times in my life, is that I might, through my words or gestures, be interpreted as an opportunist, a "realist," "a man with his feet on the ground," one of those experts at balancing things who sits forever on the fence waiting to see which way the wind blows to safely follow it.

Out of respect for freedom I have always deliberately refused its distortion. Freedom is not the absence of limits. What I have sought always is to live the tension, the contradiction, between authority and freedom so as to maintain respect for both. To separate them is to provoke the infraction of one or the other.

It's interesting to note how people who are fond of being authoritarian often think of the respect that is indispensable for freedom as a sort of incorrigible taste for the spontaneous. And those who imagine freedom to have no limits are forever discovering authoritarianism in every legitimate manifestation of authority. The undoubtedly correct position, though the most difficult, is the democratic one, coherent in its utopian pursuit of solidarity and equality. Here, it is not possible to have authority without freedom or vice versa.

Decision Making That Is
Aware and Conscientious

Let's return to the principal topic I have been discussing in this text: namely, education, that specifically human act of intervening in the world. We need to be clear that the term "intervention" is being used here without any semantic restriction. When I speak of education as intervention, I refer both to the aspiration for radical changes in society in such areas as economics, human relations, property, the right to employment, to land, to education, and to health, and to the reactionary position whose aim is to immobilize history and maintain an unjust socio-economic and cultural order.

These forms of intervention, which frequently alternate between one and the other, often encounter us divided in our choices and far from consistent between our actions and what we profess. It is rare, for example, that we perceive the aggressive incoherence that exists between our progressive statements and our disastrously elitist style of being intellectuals. And what can be said of educators who consider themselves progressive yet engage in a pedagogico-political practice that is highly authoritarian? For this reason, in *Teachers as Cultural Workers: Letters to Those Who Dare Teach* I insisted on the need to create in our teaching practice the virtue of coherence, among other virtues. There is nothing that so damages a so-called progressive teacher as much as a racist attitude, a racist modus vivendi. It's interesting to observe how much more coherence exists among authoritarian intellectuals, whether of the right or the left. It is rare to come across one who respects or stimulates critical curiosity in their students, the taste of adventure. Rarely do they deliberately contribute to the building of a solid autonomy in their students. In general they insist on depositing in their students, who are accustomed to passivity, an outline of contents instead of challenging them to learn the substance of these contents, which are in essence gnostic.

Education as a specifically human action has a "directive" vocation, that is, it addresses itself to dreams, ideals, utopias, objectives, to what I have been calling the "political" nature of education. In other words, the quality of being political is inherent in its essence. In fact, neutrality in education is impossible. Not impossible because irresponsible or subversive teachers so determined or because some teacher or another decided so. Whoever thinks "it is the work of some educator, more given to activism than anything else" has a very warped notion of what "political" means.

The real roots of the political nature of education are to be found in the educability of the human person. This educability, in turn, is grounded in the radical unfinishedness of the human condition and in our consciousness of this unfinished state. Being unfinished and therefore historical, conscious of our unfinishedness, we are necessarily ethical because we have to decide. To take options. Our historical unfinishedness demands it. It opens up space that we can occupy with ethically grounded attitudes, which can in practice be subverted. We can only be ethical, as I have said before, if we are able to be unethical. To transgress.

If education were neutral, there could be no difference between people in their individual or social contexts, whether that be their style of politics or their value systems. For example, here in Brazil, it would be necessary that everyone regard starvation and misery both in Brazil and in the world at large as an end-of-the-century inevitability. It would also be necessary that there be uniformity of thought and action to confront and overcome the problem. In fact, if education were not essentially political, it would mean that the world would not be really human. There is a total incompatibility between, on the one hand, the human world of speech, perception, intelligibility, communicability, action, observation, comparison, verification, search, choice, decision, rupture, ethics, and the possibility of transgression and, on the other, neutrality, whatever the issue.

What ought to guide me is not the question of neutrality in education but respect, at all costs, for all those involved in education. Respect for teachers on the part of school administrations, whether public or private. Respect among teachers and students. And respect between both. This respect is what I should fight for, without ceasing. For the right to be respected and for the duty I have to confront those who belittle me. For the right that you, the reader, have to be who you are, but not ever for the rights of this colorless, tasteless thing that is neutrality. What is my neutrality, if not a comfortable and perhaps hypocritical way of avoiding any choice or even hiding my fear of denouncing injustice. To wash my hands in the face of oppression.

Knowing How to Listen

One of the signs of the times that frightens me is this: the insistence, in the name of democracy, freedom, and efficacy, on asphyxiating freedom itself and, by extension, creativity and a taste for the adventure of the spirit. The freedom that moves us, that makes us take risks, is being subjugated to a process of standardization of formulas and models in relation to which we are evaluated.

Obviously we are not speaking here of that kind of truculent suffocation practiced by a despotic king on his subjects, by a feudal lord on his serfs, by a colonizer over those colonized, by the owner of a factory on the workers, or by an authoritarian state on its citizens. We are speaking of that invisible power of alienating domestication, which attains a degree of extraordinary efficiency in what I have been calling the bureaucratizing of the mind. It is a state of refined estrangement, of the mind's abdication of its own essential self, of a loss of consciousness of the body, of a "mass production" of the individual, and of conformity in the face of situations considered to be irreversible because of destiny.

Those who always see events as faits accomplis, as things that happen because they had to happen, live history as determinism and not as possibility.[1] It is the position of those who consider themselves to be totally powerless in the face of the omnipotence of the facts. Facts that not only happened because they had to happen but facts that cannot be redirected or altered. Such a mechanistic way of understanding history offers no place for the decision making that is essentially human. To the degree that the historical past is not "problematized" so as to be critically understood, tomorrow becomes simply *the* perpetuation of today. Something that will be because it will be, inevitably. To that degree, there is no room for choice. There is only room for well-behaved submission to fate. Today. Tomorrow. Always.

For example, globalization is inevitable. Nothing can be done about it. It must happen because, mysteriously, that is how destiny has arranged things. So, we must accept what in essence only strengthens the control by powerful elites and fragments and pulverizes the power of the marginalized, making them even more impotent. Prisoners of fate. There is nothing left to do except bow our heads humbly and thank God that we are still alive. Thank God. And perhaps globalization too.

I have always rejected fatalism. I prefer rebelliousness because it affirms my status as a person who has never given in to the manipulations and strategies designed to reduce the human person to nothing. The recently proclaimed death of history, which symbolizes the death of utopia, of our right to dream, reinforces without doubt the claims that imprison our freedom. This makes the struggle for the restoration of utopia all the more necessary. Educational practice itself, as an experience in humanization, must be impregnated with this ideal.

The more I allow myself to be seduced by "the death of history" theory, the more I admit the possibility that tomorrow will be as inevitable as today. And therefore that the neoliberal project that dominates the world now will be inalterable. Its permanence, which kills my hope today, will tomorrow destroy my capacity to dream. Once time ceases to be a matter that I must reflect upon, knowing that I can interfere in it, the death of history will solemnly pronounce the negation of my essential humanity. Indifference to the integral education of the human person and the reductionist mentality that talks only of training skills strengthens the authoritarian manner of speaking from the top down. In such a situation, speaking "with," which is part and parcel of any democratic vision of the world, is always absent, replaced by the more authoritarian form: speaking "to." This type of speaking from the top down is in itself a clear demonstration of the absence of a democratizing mentality, the absence of the intention to speak "with." One sign of this trend is that pedagogical evaluations of teachers and students are becoming progressively more dominated by "top down" forms of discourse that try to pass themselves off as democratic.

This is why I say that whoever feels that she/he has something to

say ought also to accept, as a duty, the need to motivate and challenge the listeners to speak and reply. It is intolerable to see teachers
giving themselves the right to behave as if they owned the truth—
and taking all the time they waste to talk about it. Such an authoritarian attitude presupposes that the listener's time is also the speaker's
time. For that reason, the speaker speaks in a hollow, silenced space
and not in a space that is the presence of listening. Conversely, the
space of the democratic-minded teacher who learns to speak by listening is interrupted by the intermittent silence of his or her own
capacity to listen, waiting for that voice that may desire to speak
from the depths of its own silent listening.

The importance of silence in the context of communication is
fundamental. On the one hand, it affords me space while listening to
the verbal communication of another person and allows me to enter
into the internal rhythm of the speaker's thought and experience that
rhythm as language. On the other hand, silence makes it possible for
the speaker who is really committed to the experience of communication rather than to the simple transmission of information to hear
the question, the doubt, the creativity of the person who is listening.
Without this, communication withers.

One of the characteristics of our human existential experience compared to other forms of life on our planet is our ability to comprehend
the world upon which and in which we act. This process occurs in
simultaneous harmony with the innate intelligibility of the object of
our comprehension. There is no such thing as a comprehension of the
real without a "real" that is at the same time communicable.

The question that concerns us as teachers and students who have
developed a loving yet critical relationship with freedom is not that
of being against evaluations per se (which are obviously necessary)
but of resisting a type of methodology that aims at silencing constructive diversity, constructive criticism, and, ultimately, freedom.
What we have to do is struggle to grasp the theoretical and practical

implications of such evaluations. We must see to what extent they may serve as an instrument for enabling teachers who are critical to put themselves at the service of freedom and not of domestication. The type of evaluation that stimulates speaking *to* as a stage on the way to speaking *with*.

In the process of speaking and listening, the discipline of silence, which needs to be developed with serious intent by subjects who speak and listen, is a sine qua non of dialogical communication. The person who knows how to listen demonstrates this, in obvious fashion, by being able to control the urge to speak (which is a right), as well as his or her personal preference (something worthy of respect). Whoever has something worth saying has also the right and the duty to say it. Conversely, it is also obvious that those who have something to say should know that they are not the only ones with ideas and opinions that need to be expressed. Even more than that, they should be conscious that, no matter how important the issue, their opinion probably will not be the one truth long and anxiously awaited for by the multitudes. In addition, they should be aware that the person listening also has something to say and that if this is not taken into account, their talking, no matter how correct and convincing, will not fall on receptive ears.

The commitment of the student, who is an adventurer in the art of learning, to the process of inventing, instigated by the teacher, has nothing to do with the transfer of contents. It has to do with the challenge and the beauty of teaching and learning.

It is not difficult to see how one of my principal tasks as a teacher who is open-minded (progressive) is to motivate the student to overcome his or her difficulties in comprehending the object under scrutiny. Essential to this task is the teacher's affirmation of the student's curiosity, which in turn will generate a sense of satisfaction and reward in the student on achieving his or her goal. All this will ensure the continuity of the process of discovery, which is integral to the act of knowing. I hope any readers will forgive my insistence, but I have to say it again: to teach is not to transfer the comprehension of the object to a student but to instigate the student, who is a knowing subject, to become capable of comprehending and of communicating what has been comprehended. This is the sense in which I am obliged to be a listener. To listen to the student's doubts, fears, and incompetencies that are part of the learning process. It is in listening to the student that I learn to speak with him or her.

One of the difficulties that continually crops up for us is how to work with oral or written language that may or may not be associated with the power of the image. This difficulty is connected to the question of how to make viable the communication of what lies at the heart of our comprehension and our understanding of the world. The communicability of what is understood is the potential that it possesses for being communicated. But this is not yet communication.

So the more efficaciously I manage to provoke the student into an exploration and refinement of his or her curiosity, the better I am as a teacher. Obviously, the student will work with my help to produce her or his own comprehension of the object in question or of the content of my communication. In fact, my role as a teacher in whatever I may be teaching is not simply to try to describe as clearly as I can the "substantivity" of some content so that the student may capture it. On the contrary, my role is essentially one of inciting the student to produce his or her own comprehension of the object, using the materials I have offered, certainly. The student must grasp the essence of the content so that the true relationship of communication between him or her as student and me as teacher may be established. This is why, I repeat, to teach is not to transfer contents to anyone, just as to learn is not to memorize the outline of some content that has been transferred by the teacher. To teach and to learn have to do with the methodically critical work of the teacher instigating the comprehension of something and with the equally critical apprehension on the part of the students.

Listening is an activity that obviously goes beyond mere hearing. To listen, in the context of our discussion here, is a permanent attitude on the part of the subject who is listening, of being open to the word of the other, to the gesture of the other, to the differences of the other. This does not mean, of course, that listening demands that the listener be "reduced" to the other, the speaker. This would not be listening. It would be self-annihilation. True listening does not diminish in me the exercise of my right to disagree, to oppose, to take a position. On the contrary, it is in knowing how to listen well that I better prepare myself to speak or to situate myself vis-à-vis the ideas being discussed as a subject capable of presence, of listening "connectedly" and without prejudices to what the other is saying. In their turn, good listeners can speak engagedly and passionately about their own ideas and conditions precisely because they are able to listen. Whatever they say, even in disagreement, is never authoritarian. It is, in fact, a form of affirmation. It is not hard to imagine the many qualities that genuine listening demands of us. Qualities that build up the practice of listening democratically.

If the structure of my thinking is the only correct one, accepting no criticism, I cannot listen to anyone who thinks or elaborates ideas differently from me. Neither can I hear the person who speaks or writes outside the norms of the accepted standard language. And how is it possible, then, to be open to ways of being, thinking, and evaluating that we consider the exotic eccentricities of other cultures? We can see that respecting differences and, obviously, those who are different from us always requires of us a large dose of humility that would alert us to the risks of overvaluing our identity, which could, on the one hand, turn into a form of arrogance and, on the other, promote the devaluation of other human beings. It is one thing to value who we are. It is another to treat those who are different with arrogant disrespect. And it needs to be said that no one can be humble in a merely formal way. Humility is not made of bureaucratic rituals. Humility expresses, on the contrary, one of the few certainties that I am sure of, namely, that nobody is superior to anyone else. The lack of humility expressed arrogantly in a false superiority of one person over another, of one race over another, of one sex over another, of one class or culture over another, is a transgression of our human vocation to develop.[2]

It ought to be an integral part of our teacher preparation to discuss the qualities that are indispensable for our teaching practice, even though we know that these qualities are created by that practice itself. It's a question of knowing whether or not our politico-pedagogical option is democratic and progressive and whether or not we are coherent in regard to it. It is fundamental for us to know that without certain qualities or virtues, such as a generous loving heart, respect for others, tolerance, humility, a joyful disposition, love of life, openness to what is new, a disposition to welcome change, perseverance in the struggle, a refusal of determinism, a spirit of hope, and openness to justice, progressive pedagogical practice is not possible. It is something that the merely scientific, technical mind cannot accomplish.

To accept and respect what is different is one of those virtues without which listening cannot take place. If I am prejudiced against a child who is poor, or black or Indian, or rich, or against a woman who is a peasant or from the working class, it is obvious that I cannot listen to them and I cannot speak *with* them, only *to* or *at* them, from the top down. Even more than that, I forbid myself from understanding them. If I consider myself superior to what is different, no matter what it is, I am refusing to listen. The different becomes not an "other" worthy of any respect, but a "this" or "that" to be despised and detested. This is oppression. To make a choice in favor of oppression. How can I be neutral in the face of a situation, whatever it be, in which the bodies and minds of men and women are turned into mere objects of murder and abuse?

However, humility cannot demand that I submit myself to the arrogance and stupidity of those who do not respect me. What humility asks of me when I cannot react appropriately to a given offense is to face it with dignity. The dignity of my silence, of my look. They will transmit whatever protest is possible at the moment.

Obviously, I am not to engage physically with a young person. A boxing match is certainly not what is called for. But that does not mean that I need to grovel before his or her lack of respect or offensive behavior, carrying the weight of all this home with me, on my shoulders, without any form of protest. What is necessary is that I put in evidence the cowardice of such a behavior by the dignity with which I assume my own physical impotence in relation to his or her superior physical power. It is necessary that she/he know that I know his or her lack of ethical values generates an inferiority complex and that the threat of physical force is totally insufficient to make me submit to the will of my adversary.

Of course, the teacher can abuse students without physically hitting them. For example, by a variety of strategies that are prejudicial to the student in the course of the learning process, such as the teacher's resistance to the worldview that the student brings to the classroom, a view obviously conditioned by his or her class and culture and revealed in his or her language, and which, thereby, becomes an obstacle to his learning possibilities.

There is something of real importance still to be discussed in the context of the teacher's acceptance or refusal of the worldview of the student. A worldview evidently reveals the intelligibility of a world that is progressively in the making, culturally and socially. It also reveals the efforts of each individual subject in regard to his or her process of assimilation of the intelligibility of that world.

The democratic-minded teacher, aware of the impossibility of neutrality, needs to cultivate a special kind of knowledge that can never be forgotten so as to sustain her or his struggle. It is this: If education cannot do everything, there is something fundamental that it can do. In other words, if education is not the key to social transformation, neither is it simply meant to reproduce the dominant ideology.

What I am saying is that I cannot make education into an indisputable instrument of social transformation just because I desire it, nor can it be made into an instrument for the perpetuation of the status quo just because the powers that be so decree.

The teacher who thinks critically cannot afford to imagine that the course or seminar that she/he is conducting is going to transform the whole country. On the other hand, she/he can demonstrate that it is possible to change things, which strengthens the conviction of the importance of the politico-pedagogical task.

The coherently democratic and competent teacher who is full of life and hope for a better world, who has a proven capacity for struggle and for respect for what is different, knows that the best way to modify the situation of the world is through the consistency with which she/he lives out his or her committed presence in the world, knowing that this presence in the school, though it is a special and important moment that should be lived with authenticity, is nevertheless only one of many moments.

In a recent conversation with friends, I heard Professor Olgair Garcia say that in her teaching experience with children, adolescents, and trainee teachers, she had reflected much on the importance of listening. If in fact the dream that inspires us is democratic and grounded in solidarity, it will not be by talking to others from on high as if we were inventors of the truth that we will learn to speak with them. Only the person who listens patiently and critically is able to speak *with* the other, even if at times it should be necessary to speak *to* him or her. Even when, of necessity, she/he must speak against ideas and convictions of the other person, it is still possible to speak as if the other were a subject who is being invited to listen critically and not an object submerged by an avalanche of unfeeling, abstract words.

Again, one of the signs of the time that frightens me is the insistence, in the name of democracy, freedom, and efficacy, on asphyxiating freedom itself and, by extension, creativity and a taste for the adventure of the spirit. The freedom that moves us, that makes us take risks, is being subjugated to a process of standardization of formulas, models against which we are evaluated.

Here, as I have mentioned before, we are not speaking here of that kind of truculent suffocation practiced by a despotic king on his subjects, by a feudal lord on his serfs, by a colonizer over those colonized, by the owner of a factory on the workers, or by an authoritarian state on its citizens. We are speaking of that invisible power of alienating domestication, which attains a degree of extraordinary efficiency in what I have been calling the bureaucratizing of the mind.

One of the essential tasks of the school in its role as center of the systematic production of knowledge is to work in a critical way on the intelligibility and communicability of things. It is therefore fundamental that the school constantly instigate the students' inherent curiosity instead of softening or domesticating it. It is necessary to show the students that the practice of a merely ingenuous curiosity affects their capacity to "discover" and becomes an obstacle to a truly rigorous examination of what is "discovered." Yet it is important that the students take on the role of "subject" in the process of production generated by their own encounters with the world to avoid becoming simply a receptacle of what the teacher "transfers" to them. Each affirmation as a subject capable of knowing reinforces one's attitude as both subject and knower.

No one can be a substitute for me in my knowing process, just as I cannot be a substitute for the student. What I can and ought to do, in the context of an open-minded approach to education, is to challenge the students to perceive in their experience of learning the experience of being a subject capable of knowing. My role as a "progressive" teacher is not only that of teaching mathematics or biology but also of helping the students to recognize themselves as the architects of their own cognition process.

The teaching of contents requires of those who find themselves in the place of the learner that from a given moment they assume the authorship of knowledge of the object known. The authoritarian teacher who closes his or her ear to the student also closes him- or herself from this creative adventure, from participation in this moment of singular beauty that is the affirmation on the part of the student of him- or herself as subject of the knowing process. It is for this reason that the teaching of contents, undertaken critically, involves the teacher's total commitment to the legitimate attempt by the student to take in hand the responsibility of being a knowing subject. Even more than that, it involves the initiative of a teacher committed to the adventure of bringing to birth in the student a person at ease who can articulate in his or her subjectivity.

It is in this sense that I say again that it is an error to separate practice and theory, thought and action, language and ideology. It is as erroneous as separating the teaching of contents from the participation in the student's own process of becoming a subject in the learning of such contents. In a progressive and open-minded perspective, what I need as a teacher to do is to experience the dynamic unity between teaching contents and the process of knowing. It is in teaching mathematics that I teach also how to learn and how to teach and especially how to exercise that epistemological curiosity indispensable to the production of knowledge.

Education Is Ideological

What is equally fundamental to the educational practice of the teacher is the question of ideology. Sometimes its presence is greater than we think. It is directly linked to that tendency within us to cloak over the truth of the facts, using language to cloud or turn opaque what we wish to hide. We become myopic. Blind. We become prisoners of artifice. Trapped.

The power of ideology makes me think of those dewy mornings when the mist distorts the outline of the cypress trees and they become shadows of something we know is there but cannot really define. The shortsightedness that afflicts us makes our perception difficult. More serious still is the way we can so easily accept that what we are seeing and hearing is, in fact, what really is and not a distorted version of what is. This tendency to cloud the truth, to become myopic, to deafen our ears, has made many of us accept without critical questioning the cynical fatalism of neoliberal thought, which proclaims that mass unemployment is an inevitable end-of-the-century calamity. Or that the dream is dead and that it is now the era of the pedagogical pragmatism of the technico-scientific training of the individual and not of his or her total education (which, obviously, includes the former). The capacity to tame, inherent in ideology, makes us at times docilely accept that the globalization of the economy is its own invention, a kind of inevitable destiny, an almost metaphysical entity rather than a moment of economic development, subject to a given political orientation dictated by the interests of those who hold power, as is the whole of capitalist economic production. What we hear is that the globalization of the economy is a necessity from which we cannot escape. A given aspect of the capitalist system, an instant of the productive forces of capitalism as experienced and played out in the centers of world economic power, is made universal, as if Brazil, Mexico, and Argentina ought to participate in the globalization of the economy in the same way as the United States, Germany, and Japan. It's a question of jumping on the train in the middle of the journey without discussing the conditions, the cultures, or the forms of production of the countries that are being swept along. And there is no talk about the distance that separates the "rights" of the strong and their power to enjoy them from the fragility of the weak in their attempts to exercise their rights. Meanwhile, responsibilities and duties are leveled—equal for all. If globalization means the abolition of the frontiers and the opening without restriction to free enterprise, those who cannot compete simply disappear.

For example, no one asks whether societies now at the forefront of globalization would, in a previous stage of capitalism, have been ready and willing to accept a radical opening of their frontiers—the type of opening that they now consider imperative for the rest of the world. They demand of the rest of the world now what they were unwilling to demand of themselves. One of the tricks of their fatalistic ideology is the capacity to convince submissive economies (which will be engulfed in this process) that the real world is this way, that there is nothing to be done about it except to follow the natural order of the facts. It passes off this ideology as natural or almost natural. It does not want us to see and understand the phenomenon as a product of historical development.

Globalization theory, which speaks of ethics, hides the fact that its ethics are those of the marketplace and not the universal ethics of the human person. It is for these matters that we ought to struggle courageously if we have, in truth, made a choice for a humanized world. A world of real people. Globalization theory cleverly hides, or seeks to cloud over, an intensified new edition of that fearful evil that is historical capitalism, even if the new edition is somewhat modified in relation to past versions. Its fundamental ideology seeks to mask that what is really up for discussion is the increasing wealth of the few and the rapid increase of poverty and misery for the vast majority of humanity. The capitalist system reaches, in its globalizing neoliberal crusade, the maximum efficacy of its intrinsically evil nature.

It is my hope that the world will get over its fascination with the end of communism and with the fall of the Berlin wall. And thus remake itself so as to refuse the dictatorship of the marketplace, founded as it is on the perverse ethic of profit.

I don't believe that women and men of the world, independent of their political positions yet conscious of their dignity as men and women, will not want to reflect on the sense of foreboding that is now universal in this perverse era of neoliberal philosophy. A foreboding that one day will lead to a new rebellion where the critical word, the humanist philosophy, the commitment to solidarity, the prophetic denunciation of the negation of men and women, and the proclamation of a world worthy of human habitation will be the instruments of change and transformation.

A century and a half ago, Marx and Engels cried out in favor of the unity of the working classes of the world against their exploitation. Now, in our time, it is essential and urgent that people unite against the threat that looms over us. The threat, namely, to our own identity as human persons caught up in the ferocity of the ethics of the marketplace.

It is in this sense that I say that I have never abandoned my first preoccupation, one that has been with me since my early experiences in the field of education. Namely, my preoccupation with human nature.[3] It is in this preoccupation that I continue to proclaim my loyalty. Even before I ever read Marx I had made his words my own. I had taken my own radical stance on the defense of the legitimate interests of the human person. There is no theory of socio-political transformation that moves me if it is not grounded in an understanding of the human person as a maker of history and as one made by history. If it does not respect men and women as beings of decision, rupture, option. As ethical beings who in their ethicality are capable of being unethical, of transgressing the ethical code indispensable for human living. Of this I have spoken insistently in this text. I have affirmed and reaffirmed the extent to which I rejoice in knowing that I am a "conditioned" being, capable of going beyond my own conditioning. The place upon which a new rebellion should be built is not the ethics of the marketplace with its crass insensitivity to the voice of genuine humanity but the ethics of universal human aspiration. The ethics of human solidarity.

I prefer to be criticized as an idealist and an inveterate dreamer because I continue to believe in the human person, continue to struggle for legislation that would protect people from the unjust and aggressive inroads of those who have no regard for an ethical code that is common to us all. The freedom of commerce cannot be ethically higher than the freedom to be human. The freedom of commerce without limits is no more than the license to put profit above everything else. It becomes a privilege of the few, who in certain favorable conditions increase their own power at the expense of the greater part of humanity, even to the point of survival itself. A textile factory that is forced to close because it cannot compete with the price of labor in Asia, for example, not only brings down the factory owner (who may or may not be a transgressor of that universal ethical code of which I have spoken) but signals the expulsion of hundreds of workers from the process of production. And what about their families? I refuse, with all the conviction I can muster, to accept that our presence in history can be reduced to a deterministic adaptation to our socio-historical condition. As I have said before, worldwide unemployment is not a fatalistic inevitability. It is the result of the economic globalization and the scientific and technological advances that lack a form of ethics that serves the interests of all human beings and not just the unfettered greed of the power minority who control the world today. The application of technological advances, which requires the sacrifice of thousands of people, is one more example of how we can be transgressors of a universal human ethic in the name of the market, of pure profit.

One of the transgressions of a universal human ethic that ought to be considered criminal is programmed mass unemployment, which leads so many to despair and to a kind of living death. Thus, the preoccupation with techno-professional education for the retraining of those who have become redundant would have to be greatly increased to begin to redress the balance.

I would like to make it clear that I know full well how difficult it is to put in practice a policy of development that would put men and women before profit. However, I believe that if we are going to overcome the crises that at present assail us, we must return to ethics. I do not see any other alternative. If it is impossible to have development without profit, then profit of its own accord cannot be the sole object of development in such a way that it justifies and sanctifies the immoral gain of the investor. It may be the utopia of a minority (which will also wither like the grass) to create a society robotized by highly intelligent machines that can substitute men and women in a whole range of activities, creating millions of Peters and Marys without anything to do. But such a utopia is worthless.[4]

I also do not believe that a universal human ethic can be squeezed into the narrow confines of dictatorship, whether of the left or of the right. The authoritarian road is in itself a denial of our restless, questioning, searching nature, which, if lost, means the loss of liberty itself.

It's exactly for this reason that I, as a teacher, ought to be aware of the power of ideological discourse, beginning with discourse that proclaims the death of all ideologies. In truth, I can only put an end to all ideologies by proclaiming a new ideology, even if I am not aware of the ideological nature of my proclamation. It is a very subtle question because all ideological discourse has an immense persuasive power. It anesthetizes the mind, confuses curiosity, blurs perception.

The following statements reveal explicit and implicit ideological contents. They are often spoken uncritically. They deserve, however, a minimum of critical consciousness.

"Negroes are genetically inferior to whites. It's a pity, but it's a fact established by science."

"He killed his wife in legitimate defense of his honor."

"What can be expected of them anyway? Only a band of rabble-rousers would invade land."

"These people are always the same. Give them an inch and they will take a mile."

"We already know what the people need and want. Asking them is a waste of time."

"He is from the northeast of Brazil. But he is a good chap. Serious and helpful."

"Do you know to whom you are talking?"

"Imagine it! A man marrying a man. And a woman marrying a woman!"

"If a black man doesn't dirty the place coming in, he'll do it on the way out."

"The government ought to invest in those places where the tax-payers live!"

"There is no need for you to do the thinking. All you have to do is vote for this candidate and he will do the thinking for you."

"Even if you are unemployed, don't be ungrateful. There is a candidate who will help you. Vote for him."

"Brazil was discovered by Cabral."

In the course of the critical exercise of my resistance to the manipulative power of ideology, I bring to birth certain qualities that in turn become a store of wisdom, indispensable to my teaching practice. On the one hand, the necessity for this critical resistance creates in me an attitude of permanent openness toward others, toward the word; on the other hand, it generates in me a methodical mistrust that prevents me from becoming absolutely certain of being right. To safeguard myself against the pitfalls of ideology, I cannot and must not close myself off from others or shut myself into a blind alley where only my own truth is valid. On the contrary, the best way to keep awake and alert my capacity for right thinking, to sharpen my perception, and to hear with respect (and therefore in a disciplined manner) is to allow myself to be open to differences and to refuse the entrenched dogmatism that makes me incapable of learning anything new. In essence, the correct posture of one who does not consider him- or herself to be the sole possessor of the truth or the passive object of ideology or gossip is the attitude of permanent openness. Openness to approaching and being approached, to questioning and been questioned, to agreeing and disagreeing. It is an openness to life itself and to its vicissitudes. An openness to those who call on us and to the many and varied signs that catch our interests, from the song of the bird, to the falling rain or the rain that is about to drop from the darkening sky, to the gentle smile of innocence and the sullen face of disapproval, to the arms open to receive and the body stiff with refusal and fear. It is in my permanent openness to life that I give myself entirely, my critical thought, my feeling, my curiosity, my desire, all that I am. It is thus that I travel the road, knowing that I am learning to be who I am by relating to what is my opposite.

And the more I give myself to the experience of living with what is different without fear and without prejudice, the more I come to know the self I am shaping and that is being shaped as I travel the road of life.

Openness to Dialogue

In my relations with others, those who may not have made the same political, ethical, aesthetic, or pedagogical choices as myself, I cannot begin from the standpoint that I have to conquer them at any cost or from the fear that they may conquer me. On the contrary, the basis of our encounter ought to be a respect for the differences between us and an acknowledgment of the coherence between what I say and what I do. It is in openness to the world that I construct the inner security that is indispensable for that openness. It is impossible to live this openness to the world without inner security, just as it is impossible to have that security without taking the risk of being open.

I have said it many times before and I think it is important to repeat it again: As a teacher, I should lose no opportunity to allow my students to see the security with which I discuss a given theme or analyze a given fact in relation, for example, to a government decision. My security does not rest on the false supposition that I know everything or that I am the "greatest." On the contrary, it rests on the conviction that there are some things I know and some things I do not know. With this conviction it is more likely that I may come to know better what I already know and better learn what I do not yet know. My security is grounded on the knowledge, which experience itself confirms, that I am unfinished. On the one hand, this knowledge reveals to me my ignorance, but on the other hand, it reveals to me that there is much I may still come to know.

I feel myself secure because there is no reason to be ashamed that there may be something I do not know. To live in openness toward others and to have an open-ended curiosity toward life and its challenges is essential to educational practice. To live this openness toward others respectfully and, from time to time, when opportune, critically reflect on this openness ought to be an essential part of the adventure of teaching. The ethical, political, and pedagogical basis of this openness confers on the dialogue that it makes possible a singular richness and a beauty. The experience of openness as a founding moment of our unfinishedness leads us to the knowledge and awareness of that unfinishedness. It would be impossible to know ourselves as unfinished and not to open ourselves to the world and to others in search of an explanation or a response to a multitude of questions. Closing ourselves to the world and to others is a transgression of the natural condition of incompleteness. The person who is open to the world or to others inaugurates thus a dialogical relationship with which restlessness, curiosity, and unfinishedness are confirmed as key moments within the ongoing current of history.

Once, in a municipal school in São Paulo, during a four-day meeting with teachers from ten local schools, the purpose of which was to plan the year's activities, I entered a classroom in which a display of photographs pictured scenes near the school. Streets covered in mud and nice clean streets. Ugly corners full of difficulty and sadness. People dragging themselves along slowly, bent over and worn out, staring vaguely out of blank faces.

Just behind me there were two teachers commenting on what most touched them in these scenes. One of them said suddenly, "I have taught here for ten years but I know nothing of the immediate surroundings of this school. Now, looking at these photographs[5] and seeing the local context in which I am teaching, I realize how precarious must be the education that I am providing when I do not even know the socio-geographical context within which this school is situated."

The education of teachers ought to insist on the necessity of this kind of knowledge, on the obvious importance of teachers knowing the ecological, social, and economic context of the place in which they live and teach. It is insufficient to have only a theoretical knowledge of this context. We must also add the concrete knowledge of the reality in which the teachers work. There is no doubt in my mind that the material conditions under which the students live give them the wherewithal to comprehend their own environment as well as the capacity to learn and to confront challenges. But, as a teacher, I must open myself to the world of these students with whom I share my pedagogical adventure. I must become acquainted with their way of being in the world, if not become intimately acquainted then at least become less of a stranger to it. And the diminution of the distance between the hostile reality in which my students live and my own strangeness to it is not just a simple question of geography. My openness to a world that is life-denying as far as my students are concerned becomes a challenge for me to place myself on their side in support of their right to be. And going to live in a ghetto will not necessarily prove to them that I am on their side in the struggle. It might even lead to a weakening of my capacity to be really effective on their behalf.

The essence of my ethico-political choice is my consciously taken option to intervene in the world. It is what Amílcar Cabral called "class suicide" and to what I referred in *Pedagogy of the Oppressed* as a resurrection during Easter. In fact, I only diminish the distance between myself and those who are exploited by the injustices imposed upon them when, convinced that a just world is a dream worth striving for, I struggle for a radical change in the way things are rather than simply wait for it to arrive because someone said it will arrive someday. I diminish the distance between myself and the misery of the exploited not with raving, sectarian diatribes, which are not only ineffectual but also make my attempts at communicating with the oppressed even more difficult. In relation to my students, I diminish the distance that separates me from the adverse conditions of their lives to the degree that I help them to learn. It does not matter whether it is learning to be a mechanic or a surgeon, as long as it is a critical learning that has in mind real change in the world, especially change in structural injustice. What it cannot be is simply a learning that leads to passive immobility. The knowledge that underpins the "crossing over" required of me to diminish the distance between me and the perverse reality of the exploited is the knowledge grounded in an ethical code that will not permit the exploitation of men and women by other men and women.

But this kind of knowledge is insufficient. It needs something more. It needs to become a kind of passion. An enthusiasm capable of rapture. In addition to that, it needs to be part of a whole body of other types of concrete reality and of the power of ideology. The whole area of communication comes immediately to mind. The knowledge of how to uncover hidden truths and how to demystify farcical ideologies, those seductive traps into which we easily fall. The knowledge of how to confront the enormous power of the media, the language of the television, which reduces to the same moment both past and present, suggesting that what has not yet happened has already come to pass. Even more than that, its power to generate a diversity of themes in its news bulletins without allowing the minimum of time for reflection on such a vast array of subjects. From news of the Miss Brazil contest we are whisked to an earthquake in China; from a scandal involving yet one more bank collapse due to unscrupulous bankers, we are hurried to a train crash in Zurich.

The world is cut down to a village. Time is diluted. Yesterday becomes today. Tomorrow has already come. Everything is done at high speed. In my view, it is extremely urgent that the power and effects of the media should be subjected to serious debate. As educators with open minds, we cannot ignore the television. We must, in fact, use it, but above all, we must discuss what is going on, what is being said and shown.

I am not afraid of seeming naive by suggesting that it is impossible to bring up the question of television without also bringing up the question of critical consciousness. Because to bring up this question or the question of the media in general is to bring up the question of communication and its intrinsic lack of neutrality. In truth, all communication is the communication of something either implicitly or explicitly for or against something or someone, even when there is no clear reference to them. In this sense, we see how the role of ideology plays its part, covering over or distorting facts and situations and masking the ideological nature of communication itself.

If, for example, a powerful television channel is telling us about a steelworkers strike, it is surely going to tell us that it is speaking with the interests of the nation at heart. It would be excessively naive of us to imagine that it would declare itself to be on the side of the bosses. We cannot hand ourselves over to the television ready to accept whatever comes. The more we sit in front of it (barring exceptions like holidays when we just want to switch off), the more we risk being confused about the real nature of the facts. We cannot leave behind our critical consciousness. It must be always at hand, especially at critical moments. The power that rules the world has yet another advantage over us. It requires of us that we be permanently alert, with a kind of epistemological consciousness.

And this alertness is not easy. But if it's not possible to be eternally vigilant, it is possible to be aware that the television is neither a demon nor a savior. Perhaps it is far better to count from one to ten before stating categorically, as did C. Wright Mills: "It's true; I heard it on the eight o'clock news!"[6]

Caring for the Students

What is to be thought and hoped of me as a teacher if I am not steeped in that other type of knowing that requires that I be open to caring for the well-being of my students and of the educative experience in which I participate? This openness to caring for the well-being of the students does not mean of course that, as a teacher, I am obliged to care for all my students in the same way. What it does mean is that I am not afraid of my feelings and that I know how to express myself effectively in an appropriate and affirming way. It also means that I know how to fulfill authentically my commitment to my students in the context of a specifically human mode of action. In truth, I feel it is necessary to overcome the false separation between serious teaching and the expression of feeling. It is not a foregone conclusion, especially from a democratic standpoint, that the more serious, cold, distant, and gray I am in my relations with my students in the course of teaching them, the better a teacher I will be. Affectivity is not necessarily an enemy of knowledge or of the process of knowing. However, what I obviously cannot permit is that the expression of my feelings interfere in the fulfillment of my ethical obligations as a teacher or in the exercise of my authority. I cannot evaluate a student's work on the basis of whether or not I have a good feeling for that particular student.

My openness to caring for the well-being of my students has to do with my openness to life itself, to the joy of living. A joy that is balanced and that when fully integrated does not allow me to transform myself, on the one hand, into sweetness and light or, on the other hand, into a bitter and judgmental crank. Teaching, which is really inseparable from learning, is of its very nature a joyful experience. It is also false to consider seriousness and joy to be contradictory, as if joy were the enemy of methodological rigor. On the contrary, the more methodologically rigorous I become in my questionings and in my teaching practice, the more joyful and hopeful I become as well. Joy does not come to us only at the moment of finding what we sought. It comes also in the search itself. And teaching and learning are not possible without the search, without beauty, and without joy. Disrespect for education, for students, and for teachers corrodes our sensibility and our openness to caring for the well-being of educative practice. It also corrodes our joy in the exercise of our teaching practice. It is worth noting how much pedagogical experience itself is capable of awakening, stimulating, and developing in us a taste for caring and for joy, without which educative practice has no meaning at all.

There is something mysterious, something called "vocation," that explains why so many teachers persist with so much devotion in spite of the immoral salaries they receive. Not only do they remain, but they fulfill as best they can their commitment. And do it with love.

But I would like to emphasize that even the loving commitment to one's task does not dispense with the political struggle in favor of one's rights as a teacher, the dignity of one's profession, and the care due to the students and to the teaching space that both teacher and student share.

Having said all this, it is necessary to insist again that educative practice carried out with feeling and joy does not preclude serious, scientific education and a clear-sighted political consciousness on the part of teachers. Educative practice is all of the following: affectivity, joy, scientific seriousness, technical expertise at the service of change, and, unfortunately, the preservation of the status quo. It is exactly this static, neoliberal ideology, proposing as it does "the death of history," that converts tomorrow into today by insisting that everything is under control, everything has already been worked out and taken care of. Whence the hopeless, fatalistic anti-utopian character of this ideology, which proposes a purely technical kind of education in which the teacher distinguishes himself or herself not by a desire to change the world but to accept it as it is. Such a teacher possesses very little capacity for critical education but quite a lot for "training," for transferring contents. An expert in "know-how." The kind of knowledge this "pragmatic" teacher needs for his or her work is not the kind I have been speaking of in this book. It is not for me to judge, of course, regarding the value of this knowledge in itself, but it is my duty to denounce the antihumanist character of this neoliberal pragmatism.

The open-minded teacher needs to cultivate another type of knowledge and to be aware of its consequences: knowledge that concerns the specifically human nature of the art of teaching. We have already seen that the cornerstone of the educational adventure is precisely the unfinished nature of our historical presence in the world and our consciousness of that unfinishedness. The open-minded teacher cannot afford to ignore anything that concerns the human person. Whether it is the person's capacity for physical or moral perfection, for intellectual growth, for overcoming obstacles, for beautifying and ennobling the world as well as for making it uglier, for being oppressed by dominating ideologies, or for the struggle for freedom— for everything, in fact, that has to do with being a human person in the world. And it does not matter with what age group the teacher is working. Our work is with people, whether they be simple, youthful, or adult. People who are on the road of permanent search. People in formation, changing, growing, redirecting their lives, becoming better, and, because they are human, capable of negating fundamental values, of distorting life, of falling back, of transgressing. Because my profession is neither superior nor inferior to any other, it demands of me the highest level of ethical responsibility, which includes my duty to be properly prepared professionally, in every aspect of my profession. A profession that deals with people whose dreams and hopes are at times timid and at other times adventurous and whom I must respect all the more so because such dreams and hopes are being constantly bombarded by an ideology whose purpose is to destroy humanity's authentic dreams and utopias.

If, on the one hand, I ought not to too easily encourage impossible dreams, on the other, I ought not deny a dreamer's right to dream. I am dealing with people and not with things. And, because I am dealing with people, I cannot refuse my wholehearted and loving attention, even in personal matters, where I see that a student is in need of such attention. And giving this attention is essential, even though it would be easier and more pleasurable to indulge in theoretical and critical reflection on the subject of teaching and learning. It is not, of course, a question of taking up normal teaching time. And the fact that I may not be a therapist or a social worker does not excuse me for ignoring the suffering or the disquiet that one of my students may be going through. However, I cannot ethically or professionally pretend to be a therapist even if, on account of my humanity and my capacity for empathy and solidarity, that very humanity is in itself therapeutic.

This conviction has been with me since I was young. Because of it, I always left my house with a sense of purpose in my step, to meet the students with whom I share the educative adventure. This adventure was always for me something profoundly linked to people. To people who were as yet unfinished, curious, intelligent, and capable of knowing. Capable too of breaking an ethical code because they are humanly capable of not being ethical. Although I never idealized educative practice as something fit only for angels, I was always totally convinced that it is worthwhile to struggle against the derivations and prejudices that prevent us from being something more than we are at any given moment. Obviously, what helped me to hold on to this certainty was an understanding that enhances the role of subjectivity and its capacity to compare, to analyze, to evaluate, to decide, and to break with the past, all of which make history both ethical and political.

It is this perception of men and women as people "programmed" to learn and therefore to teach, to know, and to intervene that makes me understand educative practice as a permanent exercise in favor of the production of intellectual thought and of the development of the autonomy of both teachers and students. As a strictly human experience, I could never treat education as something cold, mental, merely technical, and without soul, where feelings, sensibility, desires, and dreams had no place, as if repressed by some kind of reactionary dictatorship. In addition, I never saw educative practice as an experience that could be considered valid if it lacked rigor and intellectual discipline.

I am convinced however that rigor, serious intellectual discipline, and the exercise of epistemological curiosity do not necessarily make me unloved, arrogant, or full of myself. Put in another way, when I speak of scientific rigor, I am not doing so because I am necessarily arrogant, though sometimes arrogance may be mistaken for competence, even though competence can hardly be considered the cause of arrogance. Yet I do not deny that certain arrogant people may be very competent. I simply lament the fact that they lack that humility that, in addition to enhancing their knowledge, would ennoble them as people.

NOTES

Foreword

1. José Ortega y Gasset, *The Revolt of the Masses* (New York: Norton, 1932), p. 111.

2. Paulo Freire, *The Politics of Education: Culture, Power, and Liberation* (Westport, Conn.: Bergin & Garvey, 1985), p. 103.

3. Ibid.

4. Paulo Freire and Donaldo Macedo, *Literacy: Reading the Word and the World* (South Hadley, Mass.: Bergin & Garvey, 1987), p. 132.

5. Herb Kohl, "Paulo Freire: Liberation Pedagogy" in *The Nation*, 26 May 1997, p. 7.

6. Pepi Leistyna, "The Fortunes of My Miseducation at Harvard Graduate School of Education" in *Tongue-Tying Multiculturalism: The Politics of Race and Culture in the Ivy League*, ed. Donaldo Macedo, forthcoming.

7. Ibid.

8. Carry Nelson, *Manifesto of a Tenured Radical* (New York: New York University Press, 1997), p. 19.

9. Ibid.

10. Henry A. Giroux, *Theory and Resistance: A Pedagogy for the Opposition* (South Hadley, Mass.: J.F. Bergin, 1983), p. 87.

11. Michael Schudson, *Discovering the News: A Social History of American Newspapers* (New York: Basic Books, 1978), p. 6.

12. Ibid.

13. For a comprehensive and critical discussion of scientific objectivity, see Donna Haraway, "Situated Knowledges: The Science Question in Feminism and the Privilege of Partial Perspective," *Feminist Studies* 14 (1988): 575–599.

14. Linda Brodkey, *Writing Permitted in Designated Areas Only* (Minnesota: Minnesota University Press, 1996), p. 10.

15. Ibid., p.8.

16. Ibid.

17. Roger Fowler et al., *Language and Control* (London: Routledge & Kegan Paul, 1979), p. 192.

18. Greg Myers, "Reality, Consensus, and Reform in the Rhetoric of Composition Teaching," *College English* 48, no. 2 (February 1986).

19. Jonathan Kozol, *Amazing Grace: The Lines and the Conscience of a Nation* (New York: Harper Perennial, 1996), p. 4.

20. Ibid., p. 39.

21. Ibid.

22. Richard J. Hernstein and Charles Murray, *The Bell Curve: Intelligence and Class Structure in American Life* (New York: The Free Press, 1994).

23. bell hooks, *Yearning: Race, Gender and Cultural Politics* (Boston: South End Press, 1990).

24. Renato Constantino, *Neocolonial Identity and Counter Consciousness* (London: Merlin Press, 1978).

25. Albert Memmi, *The Colonizer and the Colonized* (Boston: Beacon Press, 1965), p. 26.

26. Ibid., p. 40.

27. Ibid.

28. Ibid.

29. Paulo Freire, *The Politics of Education* (Westport, Conn.: Bergin & Garvey, 1985), p. 11.

30. Vaclav Havel, *Living in Truth* (London: Faber and Faber, 1989), p. 4.

31. Jean-Paul Sartre, introduction to *The Colonizer and the Colonized*, by Albert Memmi (Boston: Beacon Press, 1965), pp. xxiv–xxv.

32. Ibid., p. xxvi.

Chapter One

1. Regina L. Garcia and Victor V. Valla, "The Voice of the Excludeds" in *Cadernos Cede*, 38.

Chapter Two

1. François Jacob, "Nous sommes programmés, mais pour apprendre," *Le Courrier* UNESCO (February 1991).

2. Paulo Freire, *À Sombra desta Mangueira* (São Paulo: Olho d'água, 1995).

3. Paulo Freire, *Pedagogia do Oprimido* (Rio de Janeiro: Paz e Terra, 1975).

4. For this purpose, see Vieira Pinto Álvaro, *Ciência e Existência* (Rio de Janeiro: Paz e Terra, 1969).

5. One talks too much, with insistence, of the researcher teacher. In my opinion, research is not a quality in a teacher nor a way of teaching or acting that can be added to the one of simply teaching. To question, to search, and to research are parts of the nature of teaching practice. What is necessary is that, in their ongoing education, teachers consider themselves researchers because they are teachers.

6. For this purpose, see Neil Postman, *Technology: The Surrender of Culture to Technology* (New York: Alfred A. Knopf, 1992).

7. See Paulo Freire, *Cartas à Cristina* (Rio de Janeiro: Paz e Terra, 1995), Décima Sexta Carta, p. 207.

8. Paulo Freire, *Pedagogia da Esperança* (Rio de Janeiro: Paz e Terra, 1994).

9. Paulo Freire, *Education in the City* (São Paulo: Cortez Editora, 1991).

10. This is a fundamental preoccupation of Prof. Miguel Arroio and his team in Belo Horizonte, where they have reinvented the school in a way that should serve as a model for the rest of the country. But none of the media seem interested in making known this experience or similar experiences in Uberaba, Porto Alegre, Recife, and so many other places throughout Brazil. It's a great pity that such creative practices promoted by people willing to take risks, whether in private or public schools, are so marginalized when they could be the subject of a television program of considerable impact.

Chapter Three

1. See Freire, *Pedagogia da Esperança*, and Freire, *À Sombra desta Mangueira*.

2. Jacob, "Nous sommes programmés."

3. See Freire, *Cartas à Cristina.*

4. See Paulo Freire, "Cartas a quem ousa ensinar" (Letters to whom dare teaching) in *Professora Sim, Tia, Não* (Teacher yes, aunt, no) (São Paulo: Olho d'água, 1995).

5. I insist on the reading of *Professora Sim, Tia, Não.*

6. See Paulo Freire, *Teachers as Cultural Workers: Letters to Those Who Dare Teach* (translation of Professora Sim, *Tia, Não)* (Boulder, Colo.: Westview Press, 1997).

7. See Freire, *Pedagogia do Oprimido,* and Freire, *Pedagogia da Esperança.*

Chapter Four

1. See Freire, *Pedagogia da Esperança.*

2. See Freire, *Pedagogia do Oprimido.*

3. See Freire, *Pedagogia da Esperança, Cartas à Cristina,* and *Pedagogia do Oprimido.*

4. Joseph Moermann, "La globalization de l'economie provoquera-t-elle un mai 68 mondial?: La marmite mondiale sous pression," *Le Courrier* 8 (August 1996), Swiss edition.

5. The photos that were on display were taken by a team of teachers of the area.

6. C. Wright Mills, *The Power Elite (A elite do poder)* (New York: Oxford University Press, 1956).

INDEX

ABOUT THE AUTHOR

The late Paulo Freire of Brazil—teacher, philosopher, and activist—is widely regarded in the United States and elsewhere as one of the most influential educators of the twentieth century. He is the author of more than twenty books, which have been translated and sold widely throughout the world.

CPSIA information can be obtained at www.ICGtesting.com
Printed in the USA
LVOW06s0730161015

458513LV00001BA/44/P

9 780847 690473